The Columbus Dispatch

UNSTOPPABLE
BUCKEYES 2006

BIG TEN CHAMPIONSHIP SEASON

SP
SPORTS PUBLISHING L.L.C.

SportsPublishingLLC.com

SportsPublishingLLC.com

The Columbus Dispatch

PUBLISHER
PETER L. BANNON AND
JOSEPH J. BANNON SR.

SENIOR MANAGING EDITOR
SUSAN M. MOYER

EDITOR
TRAVIS W. MORAN

ART DIRECTOR AND COVER DESIGNER
K. JEFFREY HIGGERSON

PHOTO EDITOR
ERIN LINDEN-LEVY

GRAPHIC DESIGNER
DUSTIN J. HUBBART

LAYOUT AND DEVELOPMENT
LAURA PODESCHI

CHAIRMAN, PUBLISHER AND CEO
JOHN F. WOLFE

VICE CHAIRMAN AND ASSOCIATE PUBLISHER
MICHAEL F. CURTIN

PRESIDENT
MICHAEL J. FIORILE

EDITOR
BENJAMIN J. MARRISON

MANAGING EDITOR / VISUALS
KARL KUNTZ

ASSISTANT MANAGING EDITOR
DAN HUGHES

SPORTS EDITOR
RAY STEIN

ISBN 10: 1-59670-254-0
ISBN 13: 978-1-59670-254-7

Front cover and title page photo: Dispatch photo by Neal C. Lauron.
Back cover photo: Dispatch photo by Mike Munden.

Sports Publishing L.L.C.
804 North Neil Street
Champaign, IL 61820
Phone: 1-877-424-2665
Fax: 217-363-2073
SportsPublishingLLC.com

Printed in the United States of America.

CONTENTS

EDITOR'S NOTE

efore the 2006 college football season began, the Associated Press made the Ohio State Buckeyes the consensus No. 1 team in the land.

Five times before, the Buckeyes were the No. 1 team in the preseason poll. But in each of those five seasons, Ohio State failed to finish the year with their No. 1 ranking intact.

The question for the 2006 Buckeyes was the same as those that came before them: Could they keep the No.1 ranking all year and break the string?

Many wondered whether the team with such an explosive offense could be brought down by what was—at the time—considered a suspect defense. After all, the defense lost nine members of the 11-man starting unit.

Head coach Jim Tressel downplayed the No. 1 ranking.

"At Ohio State, whether you're ranked high or you're not ranked high, the expectation to win all your games is there," he said after the rankings were released.

On paper, the schedule looked daunting, including playing at Texas, Iowa, and Illinois, and hosting Penn State, Michigan State, and archrival Michigan.

On November 18, the Buckeyes finished running the table, ending the preseason jinx that had plagued previous teams. Led by Heisman finalist Troy Smith, Ohio State went 12-0 in the regular season, earning the team a place in the BCS National Championship game January 8 in Glendale, Arizona.

While the OSU offense performed as expected—with Smith throwing at will to wideouts Ted Ginn Jr.,

Anthony Gonzalez, and a staple of other sure-handed receivers—the defense surprised the nation. Led by sophomore linebacker James Laurinaitis, the defense kept teams off the board, holding seven teams to seven or fewer points, making it one of the stingiest in college football.

To get to November 19 undefeated and ranked No. 1, the Buckeyes had to beat two No. 2 teams: Texas on September 9 and Michigan on November 18.

The first showdown came in Austin, Texas, when the Buckeyes sought to avenge the 2005 loss to the Longhorns in Ohio Stadium. This time, there would be no last-minute drama by the Longhorns. Instead, the dramatic plays came from Smith and Ginn on offense, and Laurinaitis on defense—including a bone-jarring hit near the goal line that led to a Texas fumble.

The game of the year—some say the biggest game ever—took place at Ohio Stadium on November 18, the day after legendary Michigan head coach Bo Schembechler died in Ann Arbor. In one of the most entertaining and nerve-wracking games ever played, Ohio State outscored Michigan 42-39.

The Dispatch devoted dozens of journalists to reporting on the Buckeyes' perfect regular season. We're proud to bring you their story.

Ben Marrison

ABOVE: Ohio State fan Aubrey Dyer, 7, shows off her team spirit. *Dispatch photo by Chris Russell*

RIGHT: Golf legend and OSU alumnus Jack Nicklaus dots the "i" during the halftime Script Ohio. Nicklaus is just the fifth non-band member to be accorded that honor. The others: Ohio State president Novice G. Fawcett, comedian Bob Hope, coach Woody Hayes, and ticket director Bob Ries. *Dispatch photo by Fred Squillante*

ABOVE: The Best Damn Band in the Land enters through the north end of the stadium. *Dispatch photo by Renee Sauer*

LEFT: Sousaphone player Andrew Cloyes of the OSU Marching Band dots the "i" in Script Ohio. He is a fifth year Electrical and Computer Engineering student. *Dispatch photo by Tim Revell*

FAST AND FURIOUS START

BY KEN GORDON

O hio State head coach Jim Tressel admired Northern Illinois' gumption, even as he suspected the Huskies were in trouble. On the first play of OSU's second possession, Northern Illinois cornerback Adriel Hansbro crept up practically into the chest of Ohio State receiver Ted Ginn Jr. Quarterback Troy Smith saw it.

At the snap, Ginn gave Hansbro a juke right, then burst past him to the left and into the open field. All Smith had to do was lay the ball out, and Ginn was gone for a 58-yard touchdown.

"It's hard to adjust to speed until you've had to try to cover it," Tressel said after his Buckeyes opened with a 35-12 victory. "Northern Illinois doesn't change who they are against anybody, they believe in what they do, and we knew that going in.

"We knew that perhaps we could show them some speed that maybe they hadn't seen before, and that's tough duty."

Ohio State's Chris Wells (28) plows through a pile to score on an 8-yard touchdown run early in the second quarter to give the Buckeyes a 28-0 lead.
Dispatch photo by Kyle Robertson

Antonio Pittman celebrates after scoring on a 1-yard touchdown run in the fourth quarter. Pittman had 19 rushes for 111 yards against Northern Illinois. *Dispatch photo by Kyle Robertson*

Smith threw touchdown passes on the Buckeyes' first three possessions, two to Ginn and one to Anthony Gonzalez. No. 1 Ohio State opened up a 28-0 lead just one play into the second quarter and switched to autopilot from there.

For the first time in years, the Buckeyes didn't save their 'O' until October, racking up 488 total yards. They scored three touchdowns in a quarter for the first time since 2002.

Smith threw for 297 yards and the three scores, and tailback Antonio Pittman had 111 yards and a touchdown on 19 carries.

It wasn't flawless. The Buckeyes missed two field-goal attempts and lost two fumbles, which helped to hold the score down. And the defense gave up 285 total yards to Huskies back Garrett Wolfe.

But the fast start was more than enough against an overmatched school from the Mid-American Conference.

"I was hoping we'd come in here and give them a little bit better test than we did," Huskies coach Joe Novak said. "We came out like deer in headlights. It was like a tidal wave; we didn't do anything right. We got in a hole so quickly that it was a struggle coming back out.

"I know this: I voted them No. 1 in the preseason poll and I'll vote them No. 1 again this week."

Ted Ginn Jr. hauls in a long pass for the second TD of the game in front of Northern Illinois' Adriel Hansbro. Ginn had four receptions for 123 yards and two touchdowns.
Dispatch photo by Mike Munden

The key to the Buckeyes' early success was the offensive line, which was playing with two new starters (left tackle Alex Boone and left guard Tim Schafer) and a third player, center Doug Datish, in a new position.

They were rock-solid. Smith was not sacked and hardly even bumped.

"It feels good when Troy is not saying, 'I need a little more time,'" Datish said. "That was never mentioned today. It's a great feeling just to sit back there and you've got your guys locked up and see Tony (Gonzalez) and (Brian) Robiskie and even (Brian) Hartline break wide open, see that ball sail out there. It's a great feeling."

Pittman, Maurice Wells and Chris Wells combined for 176 yards rushing on 34 carries and two scores.

The Buckeyes' young and inexperienced defense was gashed at times by the shifty Wolfe, particularly on screen passes. He rushed for 171

Brandon Mitchell prevents a fourth-quarter Northern Illinois TD by pulling down Garrett Wolfe after a 51-yard gain.
Dispatch photo by Mike Munden

	1st	2nd	3rd	4th	Final
Northern Illinois	0	3	3	6	12
Ohio State	21	7	0	7	35

Scoring Summary

1st—

OSU Ginn Jr. 5-yard pass from Smith (Pettrey kick)—8 plays, 66 yards in 3:53.

OSU Ginn Jr. 58-yard pass from Smith (Pettrey kick)—1 play, 58 yards in 0:13.

OSU Gonzalez 15-yard pass from Smith (Pettrey kick)—3 plays, 20 yards in 1:34.

2nd—

OSU C. Wells 8-yard run (Pettrey kick)—5 plays, 43 yards in 1:11.

NIU Nendick 35-yard field goal—9 plays, 48 yards in 3:05.

3rd—

NIU Nendick 37-yard field goal—10 plays, 60 yards in 5:06.

4th—

OSU Pittman 1-yard run (Pettrey kick)—6 plays, 38 yards in 2:15.

NIU Wolfe 4-yard pass from Horvath (Horvath rush failed)—10 plays, 71 yards in 4:31.

TEAM STATISTICS

	NIU	OSU
First Downs	15	22
Rushes-Yards (Net)	33-151	36-173
Passing Yards (Net)	192	315
Pass Comp-Att-Int	16-30-1	20-27-0
Total Offense Yards	63-343	63-488
Fumble Returns-Yards	0-0	0-0
Punt Returns-Yards	0-0	3-55
Kickoff Returns-Yards	3-66	4-73
Interception Returns-Yards	0-0	1-49
Punts-Avg.	6-37.8	1-43.0
Fumbles-Lost	1-0	2-2
Sacks By (Number-Yards)	0-0	4-24
Penalties (Number-Yards)	4-35	3-40
Possession Time	31:04	28:56

yards on 26 carries and caught five passes for 114 yards, ripping off plays of 22, 31 and 65 yards.

But some new names made big plays for the Buckeyes, led by end Vernon Gholston (1½ sacks) and linebacker Larry Grant (interception). Ohio State had 13 tackles for losses.

Northern Illinois was held out of the end zone until Wolfe caught a 4-yard pass on fourth down with 10:27 left in the game.

"I think we definitely have the talent, you could see it out there," linebacker James Laurinaitis said. "And we have the speed. It's just a matter of correcting the little things, make sure we're eliminating those big plays."

Ohio State also realizes it needs to eliminate its turnovers. Chris Wells fumbled at the Huskies 1-yard line in the third quarter and backup quarterback Justin Zwick fumbled at the Huskies' 5 on his first play in the game midway through the fourth quarter.

"It gets a lot tougher next week," defensive end Jay Richardson said. "It's going to be whole different level and caliber of players we're going against, and we have to really get better.

"This was a solid start. I don't want to say it was a great start. But I don't want everybody to make too big a deal of what we did out there, because in all fairness to Northern Illinois, that wasn't Michigan or Texas we just played."

Ohio State QB Troy Smith sends a pass downfield early in the first half. Smith completed 18 of 25 passes for 297 yards and three touchdowns. *Dispatch photo by Kyle Robertson*

LONE STAR LICKIN'

BY KEN GORDON

The Texas band had finished playing "The Eyes of Texas" and begun filing off the Royal-Memorial Stadium field.

The eyes of Ohio State fans then turned to the Buckeyes, who came to the northwest corner of the stadium with shouts of glee and fingers pointing upward, signaling No. 1.

As the strains of "Carmen Ohio" faded into the warm Texas evening, it was obvious Ohio State had earned its No. 1 ranking. The Buckeyes soundly defeated No. 2 Texas 24-7 with contributions from their stars and unsung players alike, from their veteran offense and young defense.

> "ANY TIME YOU HOLD SOMEONE TO SEVEN POINTS IN THEIR STADIUM, INCREDIBLE."
>
> BUCKEYES COACH
> JIM TRESSEL

Ohio State halted the defending national champions' 21-game win streak and avenged a 25-22 loss to Texas last year in Ohio Stadium.

"Our guys played hard," Buckeyes head coach Jim Tressel said. "They came into a tough environment and kept slugging

Antonio Pittman splits the Texas defenders in the first half. Pittman had 16 rushes for 74 yards and a TD. *Dispatch photo by Chris Russell*

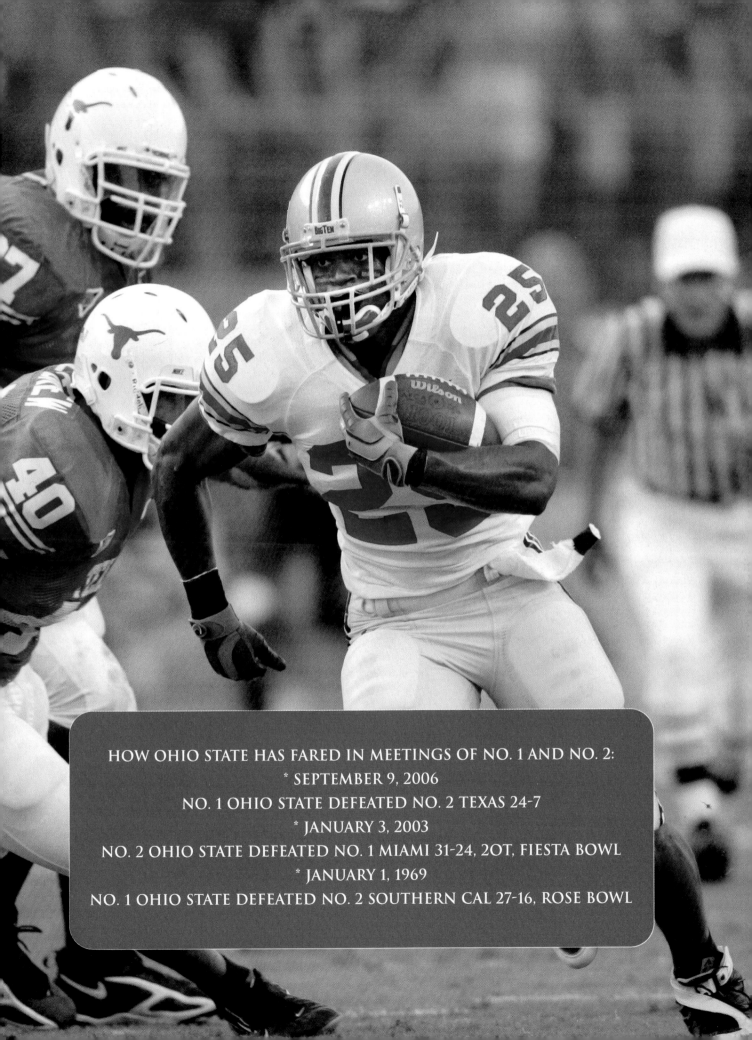

HOW OHIO STATE HAS FARED IN MEETINGS OF NO. 1 AND NO. 2:
* SEPTEMBER 9, 2006
NO. 1 OHIO STATE DEFEATED NO. 2 TEXAS 24-7
* JANUARY 3, 2003
NO. 2 OHIO STATE DEFEATED NO. 1 MIAMI 31-24, 2OT, FIESTA BOWL
* JANUARY 1, 1969
NO. 1 OHIO STATE DEFEATED NO. 2 SOUTHERN CAL 27-16, ROSE BOWL

Quinn Pitcock pressures Texas quarterback Colt McCoy in the second half. The Buckeyes' defense forced two Texas fumbles during the game. *Dispatch photo by Neal C. Lauron*

away, and our defense kept hanging in there and caused some turnovers and did a good job.

"Any time you hold someone to seven points in their stadium, incredible."

It was the Longhorns' lowest point total since a 12-0 loss to Oklahoma in October 2004.

Ohio State's Heisman Trophy candidates—quarterback Troy Smith and receiver Ted Ginn Jr.—didn't disappoint, but a lesser-known receiver and a maligned defense were a big part of the victory.

Smith elevated his already high profile by throwing for 269 yards and two touchdowns with no interceptions. Ginn, his former Cleveland Glenville teammate, caught the go-ahead TD just before halftime.

But there were others.

Receiver Anthony Gonzalez had a career night, catching eight passes for 142 yards and a score.

The defense withstood a fierce Texas running game, as backs Jamaal Charles and Selvin Young combined for 164 yards on 27 carries. Ohio State forced two key turnovers, both of which set up scores. Sophomore linebacker James Laurinaitis was in on both plays.

"I don't know anything about the yards, I know we held them to seven points," defensive

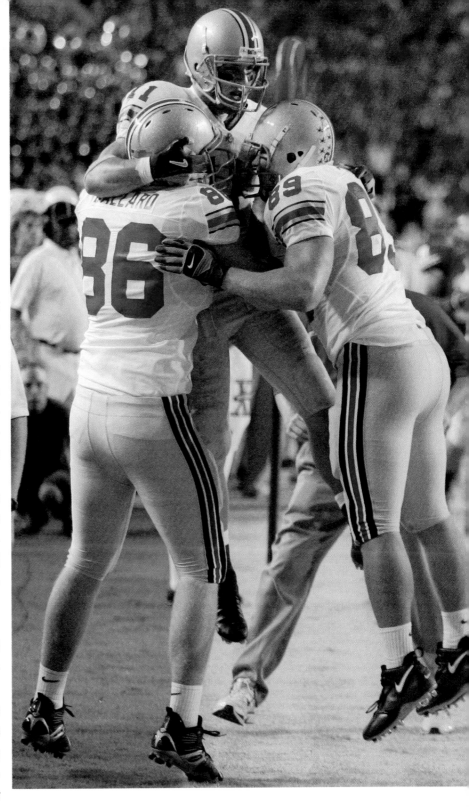

Anthony Gonzalez (11) is congratulated by teammates Jake Ballard (86) and Stan White Jr, (89) after Gonzalez caught a Troy Smith toss for a touchdown. Gonzalez hauled in eight passes for 142 yards. *Dispatch photo by Neal C. Lauron*

coordinator Jim Heacock said, eyes flashing. "I thought it was great determination."

Smith's touchdown passes to Gonzalez and Ginn gave Ohio State a 14-7 halftime lead, but it was the Buckeyes defense that gave them their first comfortable margin.

On the first play of the second half, Longhorns freshman quarterback Colt McCoy underthrew Billy Pittman. Laurinaitis intercepted and returned it to the Texas 21-yard line.

Aaron Pettrey's 31-yard field goal gave OSU a 17-7 edge at the 11:03 mark of the third quarter.

The teams traded punts until early in the fourth quarter, when a Longhorns drive reached the OSU 28. But Greg Johnson's 45-yard field goal attempt was wide right with 12:18 remaining.

The Buckeyes needed a long drive and preferably a touchdown, and they got both. Smith found Brian Robiskie for 12 yards to convert third-and-8, and Antonio Pittman ended up

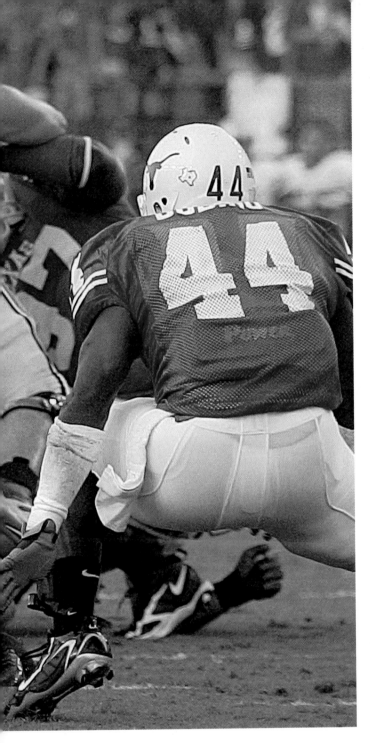

Troy Smith cuts through the Texas defense on a quarterback keeper in the first half. *Dispatch photo by Neal C. Lauron*

scoring from 2 yards out to make it 24-7 with 6:31 left to seal it.

The game opened with Texas looking like it would score first, consistently ripping off huge chunks of rushing yards late in the first quarter.

But on second-and-goal from the OSU 7-yard line, Laurinaitis punched the ball loose from Billy Pittman after a short pass. Cornerback

"THIS WAS THE BIGGEST GAME SOME GUYS HAVE EVER PLAYED IN, AND WE STEPPED UP TO THE CHALLENGE."

BUCKEYES DEFENSIVE TACKLE
DAVID PATTERSON

Donald Washington scooped it up and raced all the way to midfield.

"I was really happy with some guys stepping up," Ohio State defensive tackle David Patterson said. "This was the biggest game some guys have ever played in, and we stepped up to the challenge."

Ohio State took advantage quickly. A rolling Smith found Gonzalez for 26 yards, and four plays later Smith zipped a 14-yard pass to Gonzalez in the front right corner of the end zone for a 7-0 lead.

Texas tied the score in the second quarter when McCoy rolled and hit Billy Pittman for a 2-yard TD with 1:55 left in the half.

Smith then was masterful in leading the two-minute drill, hitting Gonzalez for 14, Ginn for 7 and Gonzalez for 23 to take the ball to the Texas 29 with 22 seconds left.

	1st	2nd	3rd	4th	Final
Ohio State	**7**	**7**	**3**	**7**	**24**
Texas	**0**	**7**	**0**	**0**	**7**

Scoring Summary

1st—
OSU Gonzalez 14-yard pass from Smith (Pettrey kick) —5 plays, 50 yards in 1:22.

2nd—
TEXAS Pittman 2-yard pass from McCoy (Johnson kick)— 13 plays, 78 yards in 7:05.

OSU Ginn Jr. 29-yard pass from Smith (Pettrey kick)—5 plays, 66 yards in 1:39.

3rd—
OSU Pettrey 31-yard field goal—4 plays, 7 yards in 2:27.

4th—
OSU A. Pittman 2-yard run (Pettrey kick)—10 plays, 72 yards in 5:47.

Team Statistics

	OSU	TEXAS
First Downs	17	20
Rushes-Yards (Net)	29-79	31-172
Passing Yards (Net)	269	154
Pass Comp-Att-Int	17-26-0	19-32-1
Total Offense Yards	55-348	63-326
Fumble Returns-Yards	1-48	0-0
Punt Returns-Yards	3-5	2-20
Kickoff Returns-Yards	1-15	1-13
Interception Returns-Yards	1-25	0-0
Punts-Avg.	6-50.8	6-42.2
Fumbles-Lost	0-0	2-1
Sacks By (Number-Yards)	1-6	3-18
Penalties (Number-Yards)	8-55	4-39
Possession Time	29:34	30:26

Head coach Jim Tressel and his team celebrate their 24-7 victory over the Texas Longhorns with the OSU band.
Dispatch photo by Chris Russell

Ginn then gave Aaron Ross a juke left and burst upfield past the defender. Smith led him perfectly, and the 29-yard touchdown pass gave OSU a 14-7 lead at the half.

"I came out, saw the coverage and made the play, that's all," Ginn said.

McCoy was largely ineffective, ending with 154 passing yards, a touchdown and an interception.

"They were a really good team," McCoy said. "We made some mistakes. They took advantage of our turnovers. I give all the credit to Ohio State."

STEAL OF A DEAL

BY KEN GORDON

After enjoying a raucous night on the town last week in Texas, Ohio State yesterday played like teenagers forced to stay home and do chores on a sunny Saturday.

Sure, they checked off everything on coach Jim Tressel's to-do list: run the ball, stop the run, force turnovers and, of course, win.

But although the score was lop-sided, 37-7 over Cincinnati, that didn't reflect the hangdog look on the Buckeyes' collective faces for most of the first half.

> "IT JUST DIDN'T LOOK TO ME LIKE WE HAD QUITE AS MUCH PEP IN OUR STEP. ... QUITE HONESTLY, IT LOOKED A LITTLE BIT LIKE A LET-DOWN SITUATION."
>
> BUCKEYES COACH JIM TRESSEL

Top-ranked OSU (3-0) started out penalty-prone and excitement-free. The Buckeyes trailed for the first time all year and didn't take the lead for good until three minutes remained in the first half.

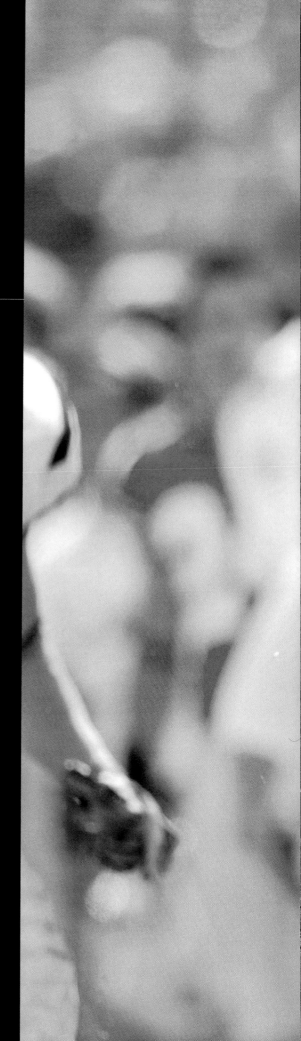

Antonio Pittman heads for the end zone in the second half to bring Ohio State's tally to 26 points. Pittman had 16 rushes for 155 yards.
Dispatch photo by Fred Squillante

Cincinnati's Mike Mickens trips up Ohio State's Rory Nicol in the first half. Nicol caught three passes for 36 yards against the Bearcats. *Dispatch photo by Fred Squillante*

It looked suspiciously like the L-word (letdown), something the players swore all last week they would not fall prey to after an emotional victory over the Longhorns.

"It just didn't look to me like we had quite as much pep in our step," Tressel said. "It just didn't seem like we were quite as explosive and flying around to the degree that we like to. Quite honestly, it looked a little bit like a letdown situation."

After pulling away in the second half, the Buckeyes could look at the bright side, such as how they forced three turnovers and made eight sacks, three by Quinn Pitcock. Or they could look at how quarterback Troy Smith connected with Ted Ginn for two touchdowns, or how Antonio Pittman rushed for 155 yards.

Head coach Jim Tressel talks with QB Troy Smith during the first half. Smith was 21 of 30 with 203 yards and two TDs. *Dispatch photo by Renee Sauer*

But most of all, they were heartened because they rallied and avoided what would have been a shocking upset.

"It was kind of frustrating from the jump because it was just things we weren't doing," said Smith, who completed 21 of 30 passes for 203 yards and the two scores. "Offensively, I can't make any excuses. Whatever it is, we have to get the job done. But we didn't whine, we didn't fuss, we didn't bicker with one another.

"OFFENSIVELY, I CAN'T MAKE ANY EXCUSES. WHATEVER IT IS, WE HAVE TO GET THE JOB DONE. BUT WE DIDN'T WHINE, WE DIDN'T FUSS, WE DIDN'T BICKER WITH ONE ANOTHER."

BUCKEYES QUARTERBACK
TROY SMITH

Maybe Smith can't make excuses, but several players said the game's early start time might have been a factor. It was a noon kickoff, coming off a 3:30 p.m. opener and a night game the previous week.

"A lot of it had to do with playing early," guard T.J. Downing said. "(The past two weeks), you could sleep in, wake up on your own schedule. And a lot of guys on the team would say they're never really morning people.

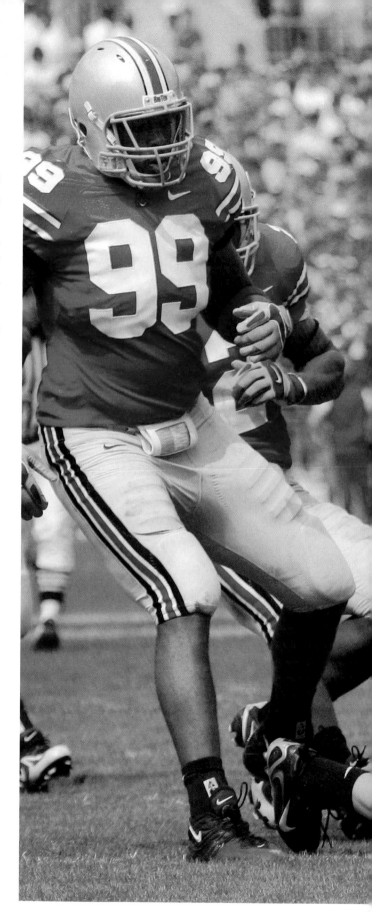

Ohio State's defense stuffs Cincinnati's Earnest Jackson in the second half. *Dispatch photo by Neal C. Lauron*

	1st	2nd	3rd	4th	Final
Cincinnati	7	0	0	0	7
Ohio State	3	10	7	17	37

Scoring Summary

1st—

OSU Pettrey 47-yard field goal—9 plays, 28 yards in 3:32.

CIN Martin 22-yard pass from Grutza (Lovell kick)—5 plays, 80 yards, in 2:10.

2nd—

OSU Pettrey 43-yard field goal—7 plays, 42 yards, in 2:53.

OSU Ginn Jr. 12-yard pass from Smith (Pettrey kick)—9 plays, 80 yards in 4:17.

3rd—

OSU Ginn Jr. 9-yard pass from Smith (Pettrey kick)—8 plays, 60 yards in 2:12.

4th—

OSU Pittman 48-yard run (Pettrey kick)—5 plays, 85 yards in 1:41.

OSU M. Wells 9-yard run (Pettrey kick)—5 plays, 72 yards in 1:43.

OSU Pretorius 52-yard field goal—8 plays, 10 yards in 4:56.

Team Statistics

	CIN	OSU
First Downs	11	22
Rushes-Yards (Net)	22-(-4)	32-166
Passing Yards (Net)	216	278
Pass Comp-Att-Int	20-25-3	25-35-0
Total Offense Yards	47-212	67-444
Fumble Returns-Yards	0-0	0-0
Punt Returns-Yards	1-3	3-18
Kickoff Returns-Yards	2-70	1-18
Interception Returns-Yards	0-0	3-2
Punts-Avg.	8-32.8	5-37.4
Fumbles-Lost	1-0	2-0
Sacks By (Number-Yards)	2-24	8-59
Penalties (Number-Yards)	6-28	8-75
Possession Time	27:01	32:59

"I THINK THEY WERE SUR-PRISED. WE CAME OUT AND TRIED TO HIT THEM IN THE MOUTH. ... I THINK THEY FELT WE WERE GOING TO BE A WALKOVER."

BEARCATS CORNERBACK JOHN BOWIE

"I think it just took us a half to wake up and get our heads out of our butts and start playing the way we should."

Until then, it wasn't pretty for the 105,037 fans.

Ohio State committed four penalties on its first three possessions and trailed 7-6 midway through the second quarter before it got into any offensive rhythm.

"I think they were surprised," said Bearcats cornerback John Bowie, a Northland High School graduate. "We came out and tried to hit them in the mouth. I think after the first couple of series they felt they were in a ballgame. I think they felt we were going to be a walkover."

Smith was uncharacteristically off-target early, but then he got hot. He completed all six of his passes on an 80-yard scoring drive, capped by a 12-yard strike to Ginn. That gave the Buckeyes a 13-7 lead.

Once again, though, the defense might have provided the key play. Cincinnati (1-2) threatened on its next possession, moving to the Ohio State 42-yard line. But linebacker James Laurinaitis leaped to tip and then intercept a pass at the 20 to end the drive.

Marcus Freeman (1), Jay Richardson (99), and James Laurinaitis (33) gang up on Cincinnati running back Bradley Glatthaar.
Dispatch photo by Renee Sauer

"They were actually having a good drive and got down there in the red zone, and James' interception kind of let the air out of their tires," cornerback Malcolm Jenkins said.

Pittman was the key to the second half. He had four straight runs for 38 yards to jump-start a drive that ended with Smith's second TD toss to Ginn. That made it 20-7.

And Pittman put the Buckeyes out of reach with a 48-yard burst around the left end with 9:57 remaining in the game.

"After that first quarter, Antonio did a good job of making things happen for us," Tressel said. "He certainly was a spark, especially the one that closed the door. That was big."

On balance, a 30-point victory isn't bad for a team that admittedly lacked focus. And so with their chores finally done, the young Buckeyes prepared to go out and enjoy the rest of their evening.

"The good thing is, our team regrouped after we kind of let our guard down a little bit," Laurinaitis said. "We came back strong, and it kind of shows the character of this team. We got hit in the face, and we can't do that the rest of the year. We've got to be up the whole time."

OSU WEATHERS RAIN WITH 2ND-HALF RALLY

BY KEN GORDON

For a half, Ohio State and Penn State wallowed around in the mud and the blood and the rain.

Helmets flew off, Nittany Lions head coach Joe Paterno walked off (twice) and uniforms gradually changed from red and white to gray.

And then the Buckeyes rose from the mire. Scoring by land and by air, with two defensive scores to cap it off, top-ranked Ohio State ran its win streak to 11 with a 28-6 victory that can only be termed gritty.

"I think this was the funnest game I've played so far because of their physicalness and their toughness," Buckeyes defensive tackle David Patterson said. "They really challenged our heart and our will."

It wasn't a day for OSU's usual big-play suspects. Quarterback Troy Smith (12 of 22, 115 yards) threw his first interceptions since last November. Receivers Ted Ginn Jr. and Anthony Gonzalez combined for four catches for 31 yards.

Trailing 3-0 at the half, Ohio State (4-0, 1-0) got a big second half from running back Antonio Pittman (110 yards and a touchdown), a big play from Smith to Brian Robiskie, and a big goal-line stand and two interception-return TDs from its defense.

Chris Wells (28) and Antonio Pittman (25) celebrate after Pittman scored in the second half. Pittman rushed 20 times for 110 yards. *Dispatch photo by Renee Sauer*

Malcolm Jenkins (2) heads for the end zone after intercepting Penn State QB Anthony Morelli's pass in the third quarter and returning it 61 yards for the score. *Dispatch photo by Fred Squillante*

"Our kids kept playing, they never stopped fighting," Buckeyes head coach Jim Tressel said. "In the Big Ten, it's always four-quarter games, and we won the four-quarter game."

Penn State (2-2, 0-1) played its typical hard-nose style. Linebacker Paul Posluszny was sent off to change uniforms after a cut soaked his forearm with blood, and Paterno made two in-game trips to the locker room to take care of what he termed gastrointestinal disease.

But quarterback Anthony Morelli threw three interceptions, wasting a fine game by tailback Tony Hunt (135 yards), and Kevin Kelly missed a field goal attempt.

In the end, the Nittany Lions left Columbus winless in their last seven tries here, a span in which they have not topped 10 points.

"I thought we played well on both sides of the football except for those big mistakes," said Paterno, who finished the game on the sideline. "I have no complaints, but you can't give up big plays."

Ohio State head coach Jim Tressel meets with Penn State head coach Joe Paterno at midfield before their game.
Dispatch photo by Karl Kuntz

SEPTEMBER 23, 2006 • BUCKEYES 28, NITTANY LIONS 6

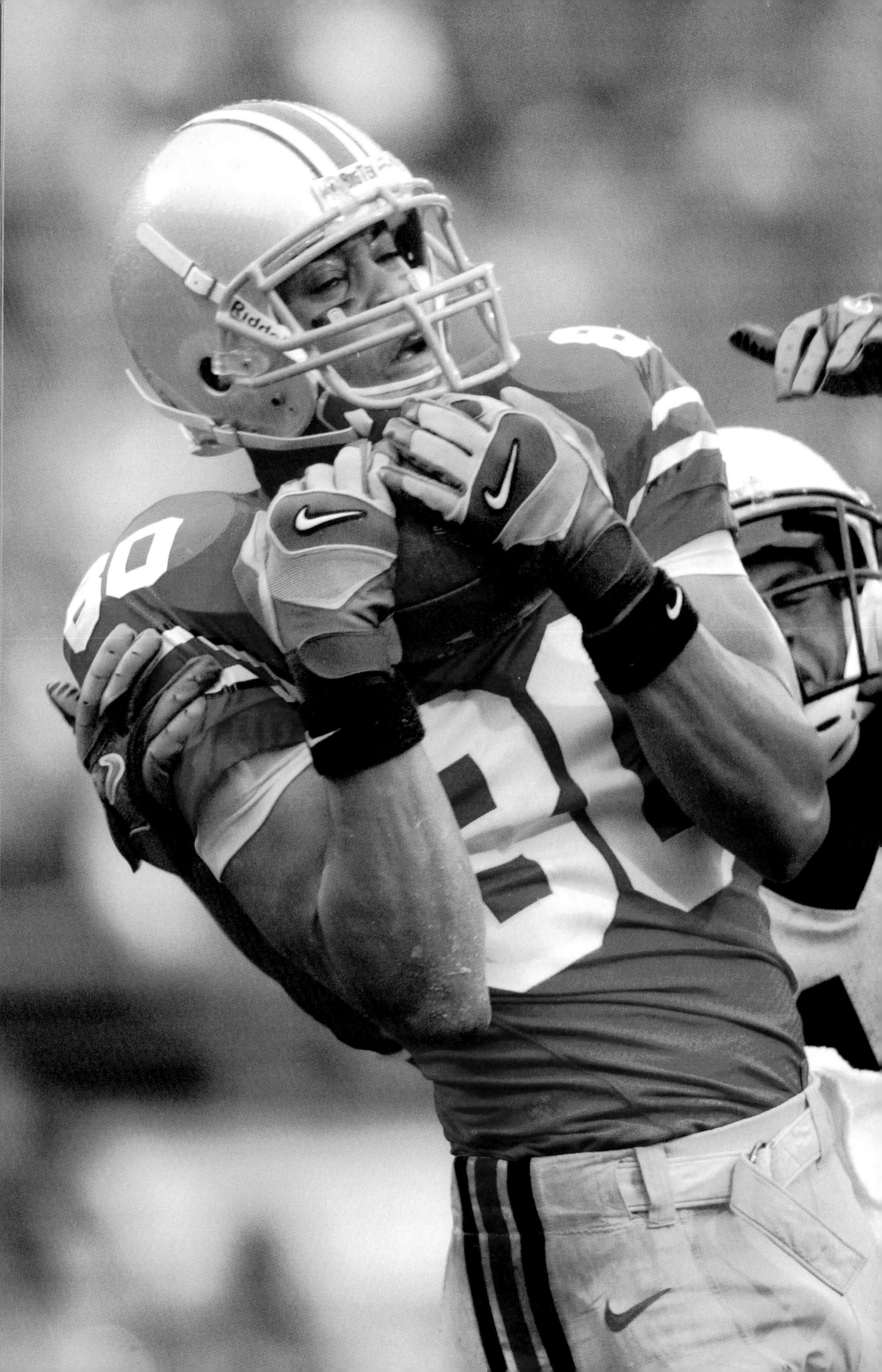

"THEY REALLY CHALLENGED OUR HEART AND OUR WILL."

BUCKEYES DEFENSIVE TACKLE
DAVID PATTERSON

At halftime, Ohio State had six first downs and 99 yards. The defense kept the Buckeyes in the game, though, surrendering just 84 first-half yards and a field goal.

"Our whole thing is we can keep our offense in the game if it's close; we have full confidence in them," said linebacker James Laurinaitis, who had his third interception of the year. "We know if we keep it close enough that they're going to put points on the board, and they did that today."

Coming out of the locker room, Ohio State turned to Pittman. His 19-yard run and 17-yard catch helped the Buckeyes reach the Penn State 12. The Buckeyes then caught Penn State in a blitz, and Pittman veered into the end zone for a 7-3 lead with 9:06 left in the third quarter.

"(Fullback) Stan White had to make a key block early back in the backfield," Pittman said. "The safety shot the gap and I had to turn it up."

That seemed to relax the Buckeyes, who turned in their most dazzling offensive play early in the fourth quarter.

On second-and-9 from the Penn State 37, Smith was flushed out of the pocket to his right. He did a 180-degree spin back left to avoid end Tim Shaw. On the run, Smith fired to the end zone, where Robiskie had a step on cornerback Tony Davis and laid out to catch it for a 14-3 lead.

Brian Robiskie (80) pulls in a 37-yard touchdown pass from Troy Smith in front of Penn State's Tony Davis in the fourth quarter.
Dispatch photo by Fred Squillante

	1st	2nd	3rd	4th	Final
Penn State	0	3	0	3	6
Ohio State	0	0	7	21	28

Scoring Summary
2nd—
PSU Kelly 21-yard field goal—11 plays, 67 yards in 5:58.

3rd—
OSU Pittman 12-yard run (Pettrey kick)—9 plays, 75 yards in 3:30.

4th—
OSU Robiskie 37-yard pass from Smith (Pettrey kick)—7 plays, 62 yards in 3:38.

PSU Kelly 23-yard field goal—10 plays, 74 yards in 5:23.

OSU Jenkins 61-yard interception return (Pettrey kick).

OSU A.Smith 55-yard interception return (Pretorius kick).

Team Statistics

	PSU	OSU
First Downs	16	14
Rushes-Yards (Net)	40-142	29-138
Passing Yards (Net)	106	115
Pass Comp-Att-Int	16-25-3	12-22-2
Total Offense Yards	65-248	51-253
Fumble Returns-Yards	0-0	0-0
Punt Returns-Yards	1-0	3-29
Kickoff Returns-Yards	3-45	2-44
Interception Returns-Yards	2-0	3-129
Punts-Avg.	6-50.5	5-38.2
Fumbles-Lost	2-0	0-0
Sacks By (Number-Yards)	0-0	3-18
Penalties (Number-Yards)	3-20	6-51
Possession Time	35:12	24:48

It was one of those improvisational plays that Tressel said "better be a touchdown."

"Sometimes there's moments where you just feel like you need to do something," Tressel said. "And to take someone's instincts from him. … Sometimes when you're out in the fray, you have to play."

Paterno thought that was the back breaker, but his Nittany Lions still had some fight left.

Hunt pounded it eight straight times on their next possession, moving 70 yards to the OSU 1. On third down from there, fullback Brandon Snow was stuffed for no gain by Laurinaitis and Brandon Mitchell.

On fourth down, heading into the south end zone filled with screaming red-clad fans, guard Rich Ohrnberger jumped for a 5-yard penalty.

Kelly's 23-yard field goal made it 14-6 with 7:33 left.

"I think it was the guys finally just saying, 'You know, we're going to put our cleats in the ground and we're going to stop them,'" defensive tackle Quinn Pitcock said.

Malcolm Jenkins and Antonio Smith ran back pickoffs for TDs in the final 2:31. Afterward, a very satisfied Pitcock sat in a uniform stained and wet, with the seams starting to come apart because from all the hitting. But he was smiling.

It was a day suited for ducks and defensive lineman.

"That's the great thing about the Big Ten: I've always thought it is the most physical," Pitcock said. "With the rainy, kind of cold day, muddy, you couldn't ask for anything more."

Brandon Mitchell takes down Penn State's Tony Hunt in the first half. The Ohio State defense did not allow a single touchdown in the game. *Dispatch photo by Eric ALbrecht*

YOUNG BUCKEYES ARE LIKE OLD HANDS

BY KEN GORDON

Seventy thousand Iowa fans had all day to get liquored up, and now they were in their Kinnick Stadium seats, some just a few feet from Ohio State's bench, giving the nation's No. 1 team an earful.

"They always have interesting things to say," receiver Anthony Gonzalez said. "One guy had the same stupid joke over and over again."

But as soon as the game began, Iowa became the punch line. OSU forced a three-and-out, scored on its first drive to take a lead it would never relinquish and went on to a 38-17 win over the No. 13 Hawkeyes.

It was the latest example of how a relatively young team, particularly the defense, has handled everything thrown at it with remarkable aplomb.

Three weeks earlier, OSU (5-0, 2-0) went to Austin, Texas, and soundly defeated the then-No. 2 Longhorns 24-7.

"It was a tough scenario to play in," coach Jim Tressel said of Kinnick Stadium. "There was a whole lot of gold out there, and we're usually pretty spoiled with mostly scarlet and gray. And our kids just kept fighting and making plays."

The key word there is "kids." Out of 22 starters, seven were freshmen or sophomores, and another 11 underclassmen played key reserve roles.

Normally, youth spells trouble, especially early in the season and in rowdy road games. But this bunch seems different, wiser than their years.

Of the pregame feeling in the locker room, linebacker James Laurinaitis said, "We approached it very businesslike. We knew what

Roy Hall and Anthony Gonzalez (11) celebrate Hall's 6-yard touchdown reception late in the first half. Hall had two catches for 22 yards. *Dispatch photo by Mike Munden*

SEPTEMBER 30, 2006 • BUCKEYES 38, HAWKEYES 17

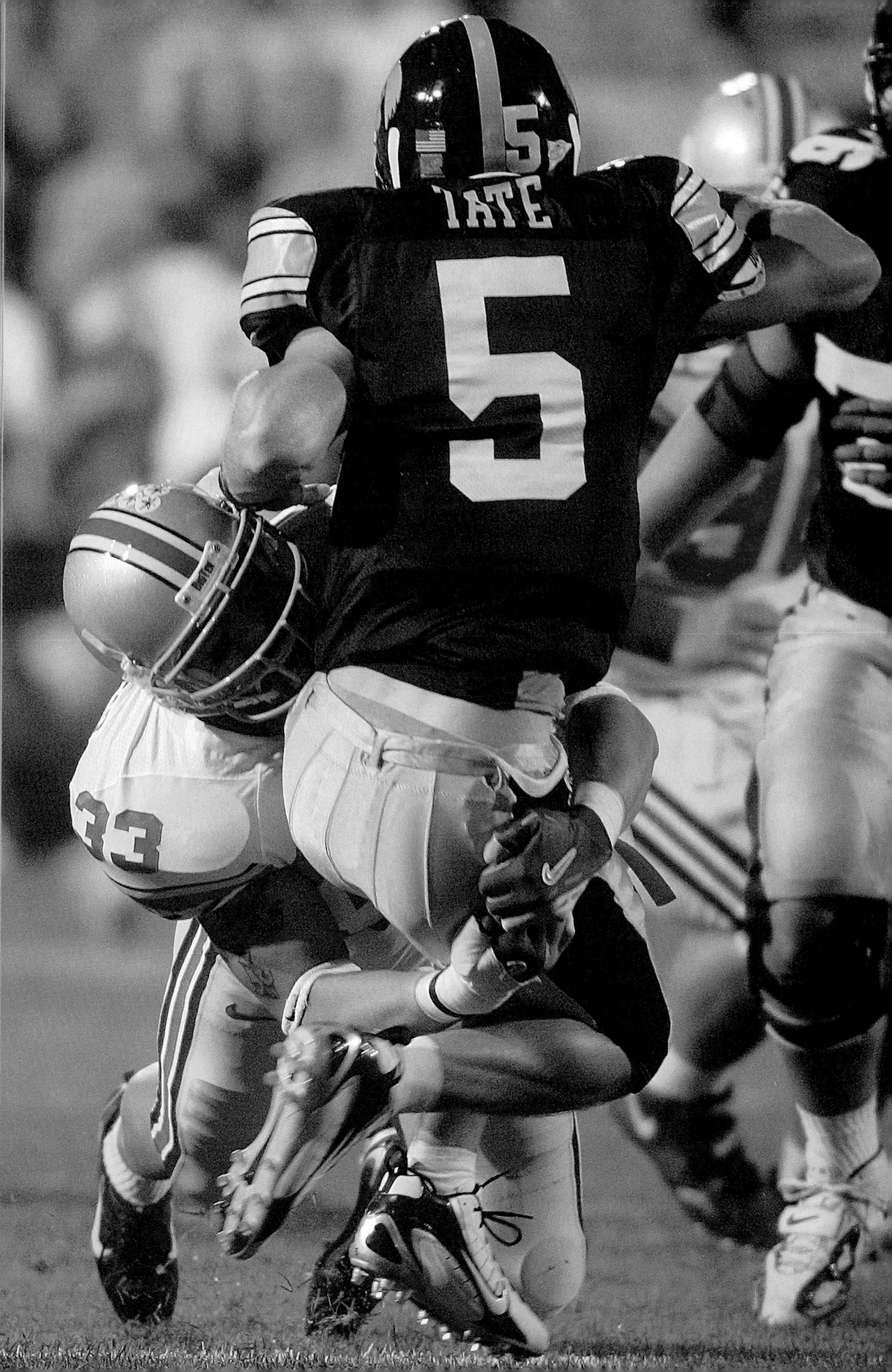

Brandon Mitchell (32) and Marcus Freeman stop Iowa's Albert Young early in the second half. The Ohio State defense held the Hawkeyes to 87 total rushing yards. *Dispatch photo by Chris Russell*

we were getting ourselves into, we knew what kind of atmosphere it was going to be. We expected all this."

Laurinaitis is the poster boy for the success of the underclassmen. A true sophomore, he had an interception, his team- and Big Ten-leading fourth of the season. He also leads the Buckeyes with 41 tackles.

Ohio State's James Laurinaitis sacks Iowa QB Drew Tate in the first half. *Dispatch photo by Neal C. Lauron*

In just his fifth career start, he talks about "young guys" like he's not one of them.

"When you look in the huddle and you see a lot of these young faces, they're not looking that look of nervous," Laurinaitis said. "They have that confidence. You kind of say to them 'Let's go, let's get a good play,' and they're trying to have fun out here just playing football."

Laurinaitis is not the only precocious Buckeye. Sophomore linebacker Marcus Freeman had an interception at Iowa and is third on the team in tackles. Sophomore defensive end Vernon Gholston had two tackles for losses, goosing his team-leading total to seven.

Offensively, true freshman running back Chris "Beanie" Wells carried 14 times for 78 yards, bulling for a key first down on fourth-and-1 behind an all-sophomore left side of guard Steve Rehring and tackle Alex Boone.

Sophomore Brian Robiskie has caught touchdowns in each of the past two games.

> "IT WAS A TOUGH SCENARIO TO PLAY IN. THERE WAS A WHOLE LOT OF GOLD OUT THERE, AND WE'RE USUALLY PRETTY SPOILED WITH MOSTLY SCARLET AND GRAY. AND OUR KIDS JUST KEPT FIGHTING AND MAKING PLAYS."
>
> BUCKEYES COACH JIM TRESSEL

And kicker Aaron Pettrey and punter A.J. Trapasso are underclassmen.

The key is, all these players don't play young.

"The biggest thing I've learned is a lot of these younger guys are very mature," senior defensive tackle Quinn Pitcock said. "They're able to go through the rookie mistakes and kind of just sit back. I think it goes with us (the seniors); we're kind of

Antonio Pittman speeds past the Iowa defense in the first half. Pittman finished the game with 25 rushes for 122 yards and a touchdown. *Dispatch photo by Chris Russell*

	1st	2nd	3rd	4th	Final
Ohio State	**7**	**14**	**7**	**10**	**38**
Iowa	**3**	**7**	**0**	**7**	**17**

Scoring Summary

1st—

OSU Gonzalez 12-yard pass from Smith (Pettrey kick)—7 plays, 54 yards in 2:24.

IOWA Schlicher 32-yard field goal—14 plays, 66 yards in 6:15.

2nd—

OSU Pittman 4-yard run (Pettrey kick)—3 plays, 30 yards in 1:11.

IOWA Young 15-yard run (Schlicher kick)—7 plays, 80 yards in 2:31.

OSU Hall 6-yard pass from Smith (Pettrey kick)—12 plays, 89 yards in 5:09.

3rd—

OSU Gonzalez 30-yard pass from Smith (Pettrey kick)—11 plays, 80 yards in 5:25.

4th—

OSU Pettrey 36-yard field goal—14 plays, 68 yards in 7:43.

IOWA Brodell 4-yard pass from Tate (Schlicher kick)—12 plays, 86 yards in 1:43.

OSU Robiskie 12-yard pass from Smith (Pettrey kick)—3 plays, 14 yards in 2:02.

Team Statistics

	OSU	IOWA
First Downs	23	18
Rushes-Yards (Net)	50-214	20-87
Passing Yards (Net)	186	249
Pass Comp-Att-Int	16-25-0	19-41-3
Total Offense Yards	75-400	61-336
Fumble Returns-Yards	0-0	0-0
Punt Returns-Yards	1-9	1-2
Kickoff Returns-Yards	2-24	2-40
Interception Returns-Yards	3-29	0-0
Punts-Avg.	5-39.6	5-33.4
Fumbles-Lost	0-0	1-1
Sacks By (Number-Yards)	2-16	1-3
Penalties (Number-Yards)	3-18	0-0
Possession Time	40:30	19:30

calm out there, we don't get all hysterical because then we'll start making mistakes."

"THEY ALWAYS HAVE INTER-ESTING THINGS TO SAY. ONE GUY HAD THE SAME STUPID JOKE OVER AND OVER AGAIN."

BUCKEYES RECEIVER
ANTHONY GONZALEZ

Whether it's on the field or in the interview room, OSU's newbies handle themselves well. They don't get flustered, they don't trash-talk. They make plays, not bulletin-board material.

None of the young Bucks seem overwhelmed to be where they are.

"We do handle it well," Wells said. "It's just something we grew up with and always wanted to do, and that's just play football."

Ted Ginn Jr. rallies the Ohio State fans before the kickoff against Iowa. *Dispatch photo by Neal C. Lauron*

A WINNING EXERCISE

BY KEN GORDON

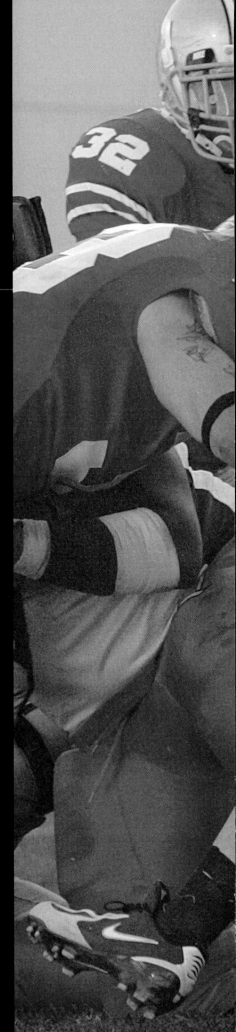

Bowling Green was already beaten. Trailing Ohio State by 21 points in the fourth quarter, the Falcons did not seem capable of mounting a comeback.

But the Buckeyes had been a little blah, just a bit underwhelming for their taste. They mostly had nibbled around the edges of the Falcons defense without taking a big bite.

Something had to be done.

On the first play of a drive from OSU's 43-yard line, the call came in from the sideline. Center Doug Datish said offensive linemen don't know all the pass routes on every play, "but we know when this one comes up."

This one was a go route for Ted Ginn Jr., who certainly can go. The Buckeyes got their juices flowing.

"We were like, 'Let's protect for a long time here,' " Datish said.

They did, and quarterback Troy Smith fired one of those photogenic spirals about 60 yards in the air. Ginn was two steps behind cornerback Antonio Smith. Ginn caught it for a 57-yard touchdown that was the final score in a 35-7 victory.

"I was especially pleased with the last one," OSU coach Jim Tressel said. "We need people to know that we're going to go deep. People need to know that's part of who we are and who we need to be."

The Ohio State defense smothers Bowling Green tailback Chris Bullock in the second quarter. *Dispatch photo by Karl Kuntz*

OCTOBER 7, 2006 • BUCKEYES 35, FALCONS 7

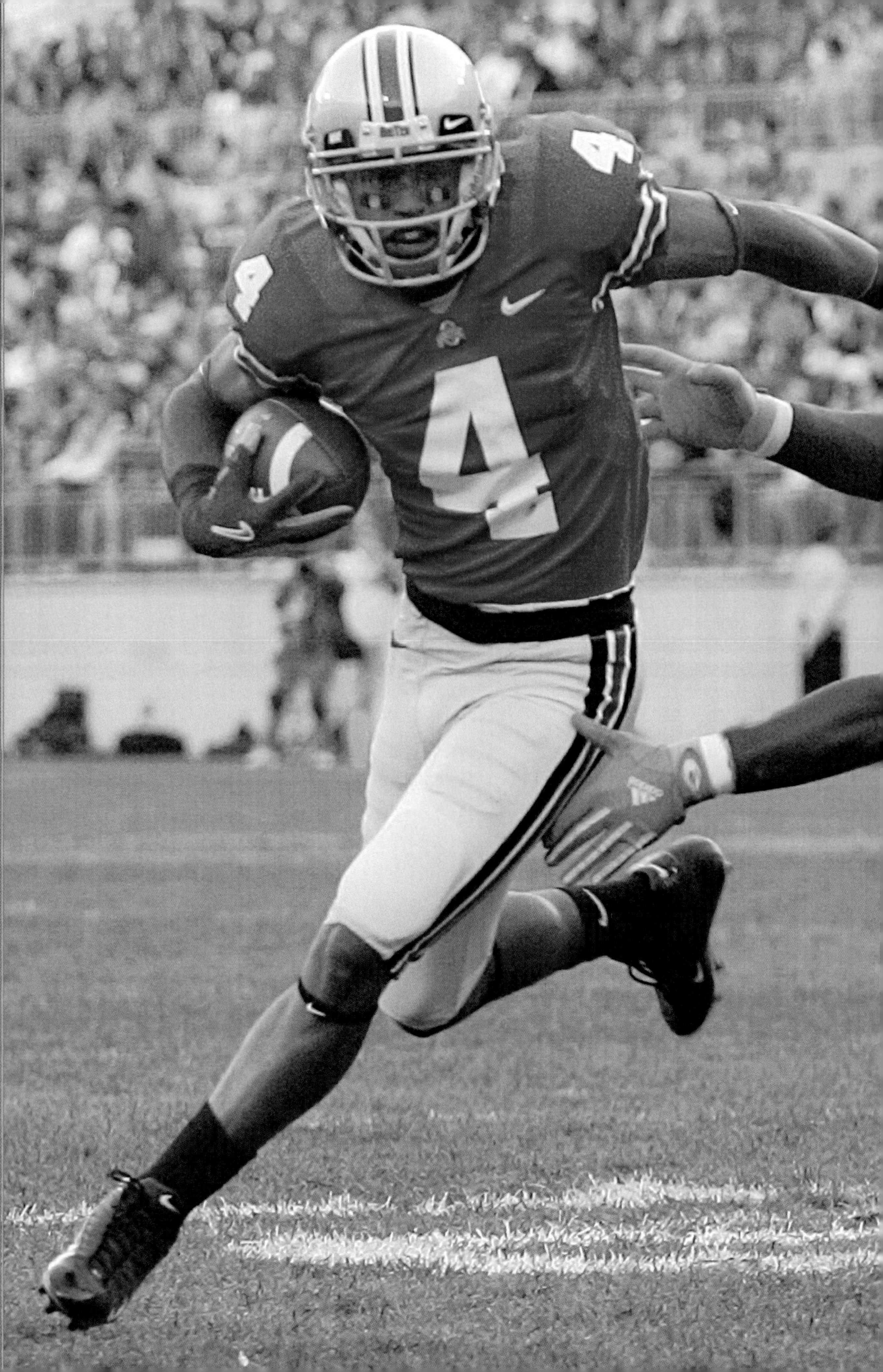

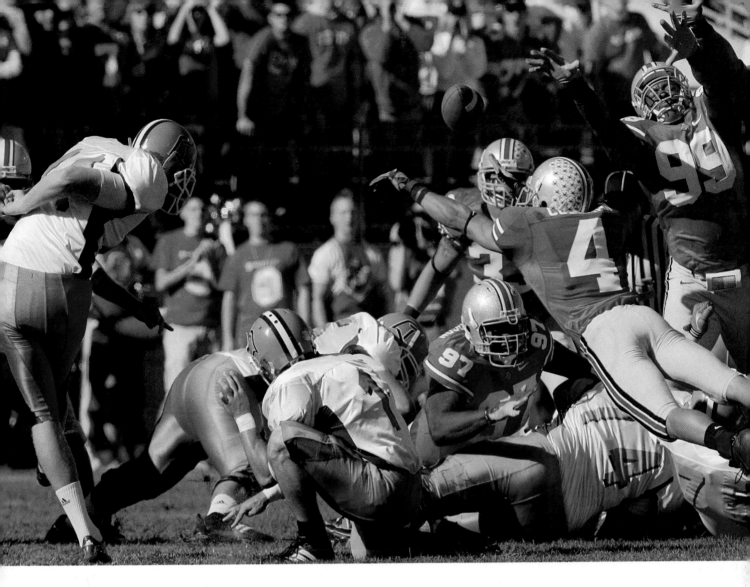

Ohio State's defense, led by Kurt Coleman (4), David Patterson (97), James Laurinaitis (33), and Jay Richardson (99), block a field goal attempt by Sean Ellis in the first half. *Dispatch photo by Neal C. Lauron*

It wasn't about tacking on another TD. It was about being not just good but scary-dangerous, about looking and feeling like the nation's No. 1 team.

It was something to settle the Buckeyes' stomachs after a day in which Tressel said OSU's effort felt, "worthwhile, but not wonderful."

That's a statement on the standards he has for OSU (6-0), which extended its win streak to 13, tops in the country.

Ray Small brushes off his Bowling Green defender and sprints into the end zone for an 11-yard touchdown reception. *Dispatch photo by Neal C. Lauron*

Smith added to his Heisman Trophy resume, completing 17 of 20 passes for 191 yards with three touchdowns and no interceptions. He also had a season-high 54 rushing yards.

Besides the one to Ginn, Smith threw scoring passes to tight end Rory Nicol and Ray Small, the first TDs of the season for each.

Antonio Pittman rushed for 61 yards on 13 carries and two first-half scores. Ginn had a career-high 10 catches for 122 yards.

And though the defense gave up 339 yards to the Falcons (3-3), it forced a turnover and gave up just one TD or less for the fifth time in six games. The special teams contributed a key blocked field-goal attempt as well.

OCTOBER 7, 2006 • BUCKEYES 35, FALCONS 7

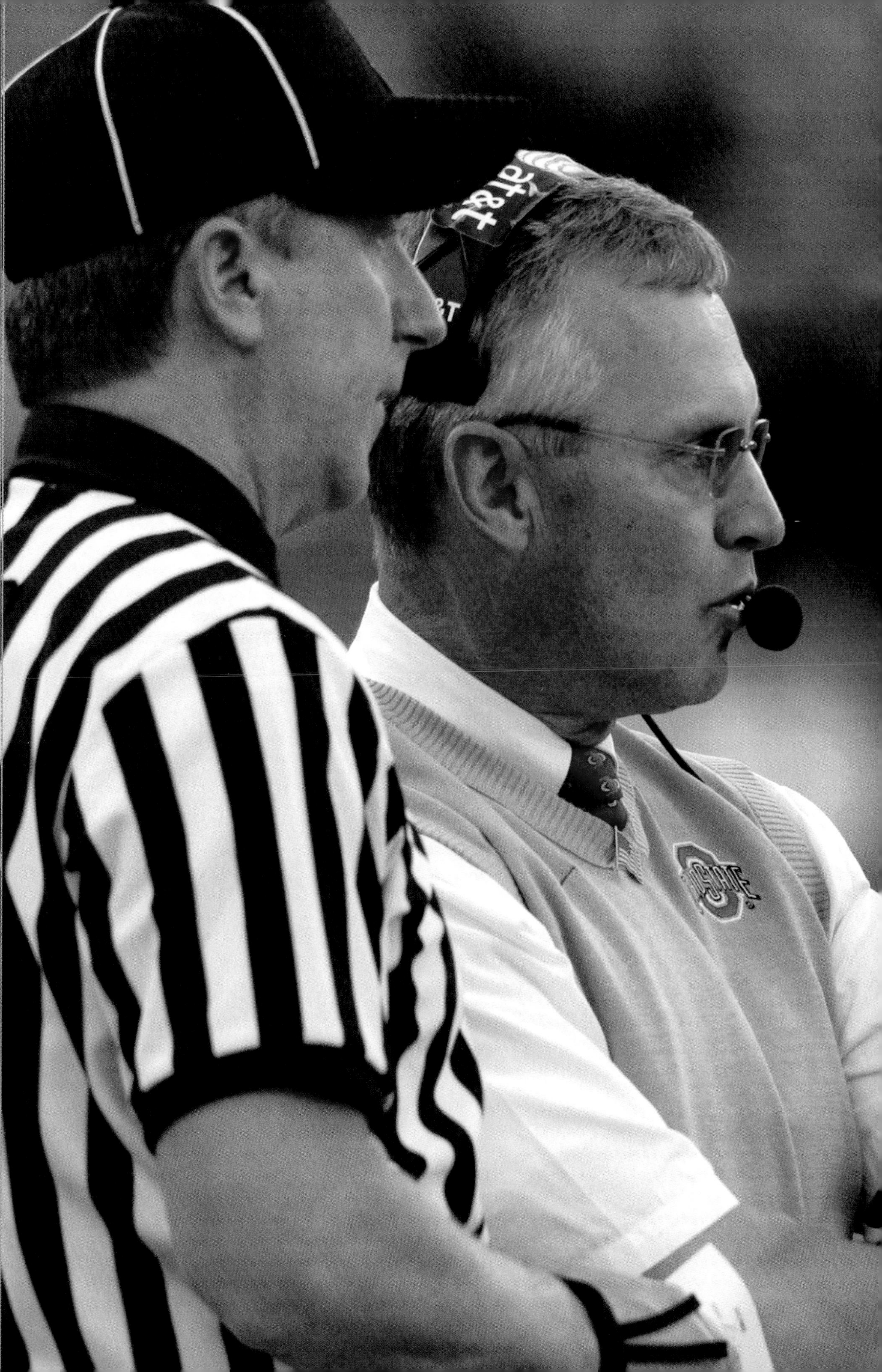

"They just have so many weapons that you have to account for," BG coach Gregg Brandon said. "Those weapons got to us like they've gotten to everybody else."

Overall, though, the feel was more of a spring game or intrasquad scrimmage. Maybe it was because it was a one-week hiatus from the emotion of a Big Ten season.

"WE NEED PEOPLE TO KNOW THAT WE'RE GOING TO GO DEEP. PEOPLE NEED TO KNOW THAT'S PART OF WHO WE ARE AND WHO WE NEED TO BE."

BUCKEYES COACH JIM TRESSEL

"We didn't do as well as we wanted, we didn't improve, we felt like we just stayed the same," defensive tackle Quinn Pitcock said.

OSU drove for a 7-0 lead on its first possession. BG answered with a decent drive and lined up for a 50-yard field-goal try, but it was blocked by freshman Kurt Coleman.

Taking over on their 47, the Buckeyes moved to the Falcons 26 before two penalties backed them up and left them facing a third-and-26 from the BG 42.

Smith fumbled a bad shotgun snap, picked it up and rolled left. He reversed field to the right, saw an opening and scooted 34 yards to the 8.

It was his longest run of the season.

"It was like watching PlayStation; it was unbelievable," Brandon said.

Pittman scored on the next play for a 14-0 lead. An interception by defensive end Vernon Gholston

Head coach Jim Tressel talks to a referee about a challenge to a fourth-quarter inteception. *Dispatch photo by Tim Revell*

	1st	2nd	3rd	4th	Final
Bowling Green	0	0	7	0	7
Ohio State	14	7	0	14	35

Scoring Summary

1st—
OSU Nicol 3-yard pass from Smith (Pettrey kick)—9 plays, 64 yards in 3:51.

OSU Pittman 8-yard run (Pettrey kick)—9 plays, 67 yards in 3:46.

2nd—
OSU Pittman 8-yard run (Pettrey kick)—3 plays, 21 yards in 1:48.

3rd—
BGSU Partridge 12-yard pass from Turner (Ellis kick)—15 plays, 85 yards in 8:39.

4th—
OSU Small 11-yard pass from Smith (Pettrey kick)—14 plays, 70 yards in 7:18.

OSU Ginn Jr. 57-yard pass from Smith (Pettrey kick)—1 play, 57 yards in 0:21.

Team Statistics

	BGSU	OSU
First Downs	15	18
Rushes-Yards (Net)	35-160	32-139
Passing Yards (Net)	179	248
Passes Comp-Att-Int	16-26-1	21-29-0
Total Offense Plays-Yards	61-339	61-387
Fumble Returns-Yards	0-0	0-0
Punt Returns-Yards	1-0	1-21
Kickoff Returns-Yards	5-86	2-19
Interception Returns-Yards	0-0	1-8
Punts (Number-Avg)	5-29.4	2-47.0
Fumbles-Lost	1-0	1-0
Sacks By (Number-Yards)	2-7	2-14
Penalties-Yards	5-43	5-36
Possession Time	29:27	30:33

set up another Pittman score for a 21-0 edge at halftime.

Bowling Green used its funky, no-huddle offense to grind out a 15-play, 85-yard drive for a score coming out of halftime, a possession that took nearly nine minutes off the clock.

BG quarterback Anthony Turner was 16-of-24 passing for 179 yards with a TD and one interception. Chris Bullock rushed for 72 yards on 21 carries.

Any hope for a Falcons rally was killed when OSU answered with a 70-yard drive capped by Smith's 11-yard toss to Small, a freshman.

Afterward, the Buckeyes were relaxed. Asked about the condition of the turf, which was replaced two weeks earlier, Tressel even joked a bit, saying, "the sideline was extraordinary."

Answering the same question, Smith saw an opportunity and took advantage.

"There were a lot of little divots and stuff out there, uneven spaces," he said. "(It will) take some time to beat it up a little bit, fall on it a little more, run some more deep routes. We'll be OK."

He elbowed Tressel. Both of them smiled. After that last touchdown, there was no reason not to.

Ted Ginn Jr. (7) celebrates with Steve Rehring after Ginn scored on a 57-yard pass from Troy Smith in the fourth quarter. *Dispatch photo by Jeff Hinckley*

Dispatch photo by Neal C. Lauron

UPSET? NOT THIS TIME

BY KEN GORDON

Their resolve grew all week. Every time they heard about top-ranked Ohio State teams losing to Michigan State, the more determined the Buckeyes were that it wouldn't happen again.

But just three plays into the game, their heart was tested. When running back Chris Wells fumbled at the OSU 31-yard line and the Spartans recovered, the specter of losses in 1974 and 1998 suddenly loomed.

"You hear all week about all the other teams that were No. 1 and lost to these guys, and we've been saying, 'Hey, this is a different year, this is a time for us,' " linebacker James Laurinaitis said. "And something bad like that happens on the first drive, and you're thinking, 'Oh shoot.' "

> "SOMEONE ELSE WILL COME ALONG AND BREAK IT, AND THAT'S GREAT. YOU'RE ONLY HERE FOR A SHORT TIME IN YOUR LIFE, SO JUST GO OUT AND HAVE FUN WITH IT."
>
> BUCKEYES RECEIVER
> TED GINN

But this is a different year and a different team, as evidenced by what happened next. The Buckeyes not only kept the Spartans out of the end zone, they pushed them out of field-goal range and forced a punt.

Anthony Gonzalez evades Michigan State's Demond Williams. Gonzalez caught seven passes for 118 yards and a touchdown. *Dispatch photo by Renee Sauer*

Anthony Gonzalez stretches for a first down against Michigan State in the fourth quarter. *Dispatch photo by Neal C. Lauron*

"WE HAD HEARD ALL WEEK ABOUT THAT, AND IT WAS KIND OF OUR GOAL OR OUR MISSION, AS CHALLENGED TO US BY TROY, TO NOT LET THAT HAPPEN. THIS IS THE 2006 TEAM, AND WE'RE GOING TO BE DIFFERENT. I FELT LIKE PEOPLE AUTOMATICALLY ASSUMED WE WERE GOING TO HAVE A LETDOWN. I DON'T THINK THIS GROUP OF GUYS IS GOING TO DO SOMETHING LIKE THAT."

BUCKEYES RECEIVER ANTHONY GONZALEZ

The Buckeyes then drove 80 yards for a touchdown. It was basically over after that, as the fired-up visitors nearly pitched a shutout in a 38-7 victory in a rapidly emptying Spartan Stadium, whose occupants were much more concerned about the outcome of the Detroit Tigers game than watching a thoroughly dispirited Michigan State crew.

"Our defense did a really good job of turning them away with nothing," Ohio State head coach Jim Tressel said, "and really, from that point on, we took over the tempo of the game."

Tressel was right, which is amazing for how early in the game the turning point came.

Michigan State (3-4, 0-3) lost its fourth straight because it could not run or pass on OSU's defense, which was missing two opening-day starters to injury but played its best game of the season.

The Buckeyes (6-0, 3-0) battered and bruised Spartans quarterback Drew Stanton (8-

Antonio Pittman drags Michigan State's David Herron Jr. with him during a run in the first half. Pittman had 18 rushes for 58 yards and a TD. *Dispatch photo by Renee Sauer*

OCTOBER 14, 2006 • BUCKEYES 38, SPARTANS 7

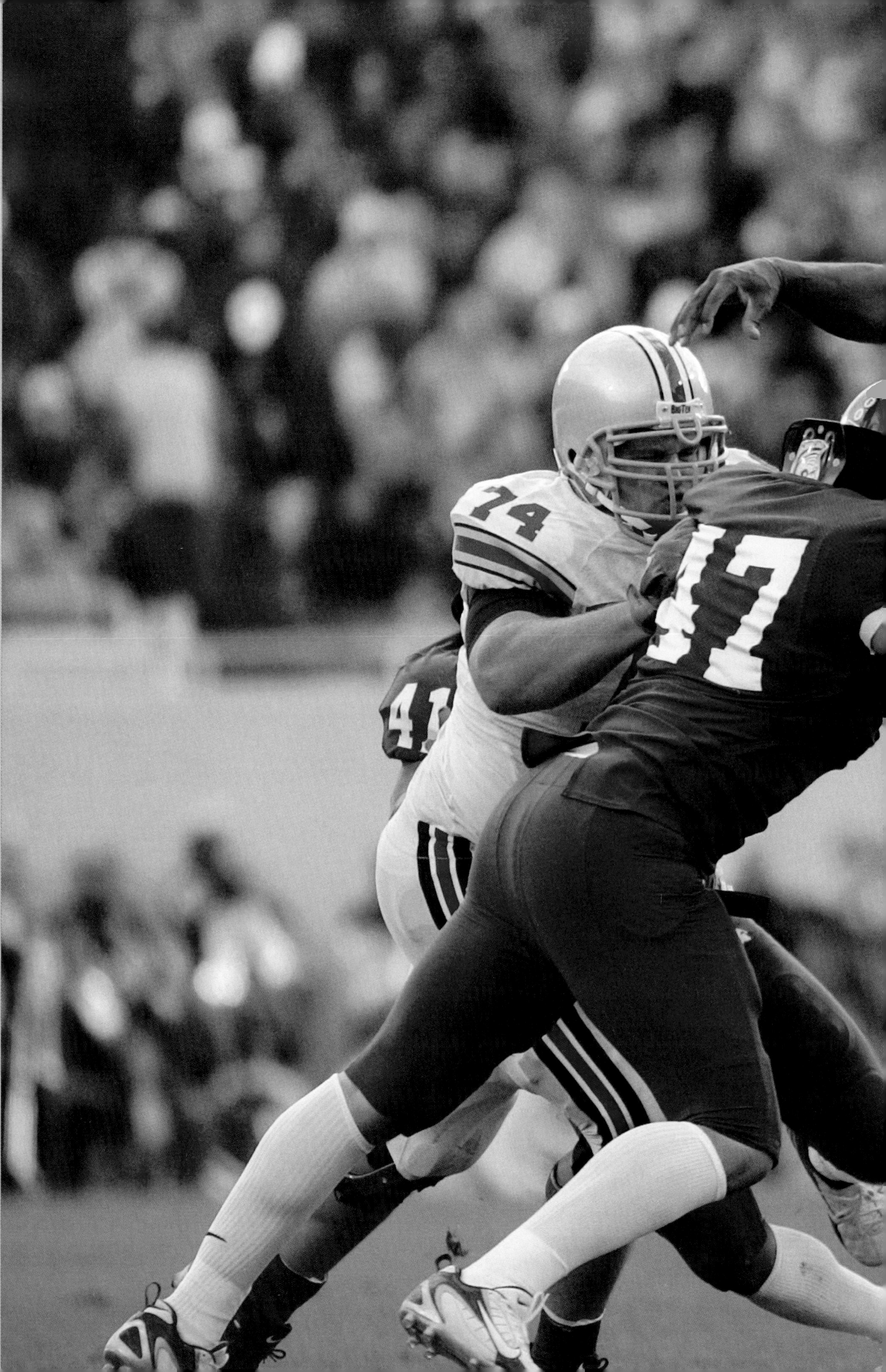

Quarterback Troy Smith's 2006 statistics through seven games:

116 of 170—Passes completed and attempted

68%—Completion percentage

1,495—Yards passing

17—Touchdown passes

2—Interceptions

of-16 passing, 54 yards and an interception). Stanton left the game after sliding headfirst into a cooler on the sideline in the third quarter.

Running back Jehuu Caulcrick also wasn't a factor (45 yards on 15 carries), and the Spartans were limited to 198 yards. Their score came when they were down 38-0, with 1:07 left in the game, ruining the Buckeyes' chance for their first shutout since 2003.

"Our defensive staff did a good job coming up with some new concepts that maybe they hadn't faced from us," Tressel said. "That confused them a little bit."

Offensively, everybody chipped in for Ohio State, which increased its win streak to 14, the longest in the nation. Five players scored: Anthony Gonzalez, Antonio Pittman, Wells, Brian Robiskie and Ted Ginn Jr.

Two of those touchdowns (Gonzalez and Robiskie) were on passes from Troy Smith, who was 15 of 22 for 234 yards with no interceptions. Two were rushing, by Pittman and Wells.

And one was by special teams, a 60-yard runback by Ginn in the second quarter that made it 17-0. It was Ginn's first return touchdown of the year and sixth punt return score of his career, setting a Big Ten record.

QB Troy Smith throws over the rush of MIchigan State's Brandon Long as Kirk Barton (74) blocks. *Dispatch photo by Mike Munden*

	1st	2nd	3rd	4th	Final
Ohio State	7	17	7	7	38
Michigan State	0	0	0	7	7

Scoring Summary
1st—
OSU Pittman 2-yard run (Pettrey kick)—12 plays, 80 yards in 5:27.

2nd—
OSU Pettrey 32-yard field goal—7 plays, 50 yards in 1:52.

OSU Ginn Jr. 60-yard punt return (Pettrey kick).

OSU Gonzalez 12-yard pass from Smith (Pettrey kick)—7 plays, 39 yards in 1:48.

3rd—
OSU Robiskie 7-yard pass from Smith (Pettrey kick)—5 plays, 53 yards in 2:00.

4th—
OSU C. Wells 5-yard run (Pettrey kick)—13 plays, 88 yards in 7:34.

MSU Jimmerson 6-yard run (Swenson kick)—12 plays, 69 yards in 2:36.

Team Statistics

	OSU	MSU
First Downs	20	13
Rushes-Yards (Net)	44-182	30-63
Passing Yards (Net)	239	135
Passes Comp-Att-Int	16-24-0	19-30-1
Total Offense Plays-Yards	68-421	60-198
Fumble Returns-Yards	0-0	0-0
Punt Returns-Yards	1-60	2-5
Kickoff Returns-Yards	0-0	6-132
Interception Returns-Yards	1-0	0-0
Punts (Number-Avg)	4-35.5	8-40.4
Fumbles-Lost	1-1	1-0
Sacks By (Number-Yards)	4-31	0-0
Penalties-Yards	5-40	4-45
Possession Time	33:56	26:04

"Someone else will come along and break it, and that's great," Ginn said. "You're only here for a short time in your life, so just go out and have fun with it."

But the beginning was what spelled the end for Michigan State.

On first down after recovering the fumble, Stanton completed a pass inside the Buckeyes 1. But the Spartans were called for holding.

On second down, Terry Love dropped a pass. On third, Laurinaitis sacked Stanton for a 16-yard loss.

Pushed to the 41, the Spartans punted.

"You get that opportunity—and you're not going to get many opportunities with that good of a football team—you need something positive to happen to you, which the turnover was," Michigan State coach John L. Smith said. "We need to capitalize on it. We lost a little wind."

Ohio State moved 80 yards in 12 plays. Pittman squirted over from 2 yards for a 7-0 lead, and the Buckeyes were on their way. Seventeen second-quarter points ended all doubt.

It also ended any haunting thoughts about a wounded-but-dangerous Spartans team thwarting the Buckeyes' national-title hopes.

"We had heard all week about that, and it was kind of our goal or our mission, as challenged to us by Troy, to not let that happen," Gonzalez said. "This is the 2006 team, and we're going to be different.

"I felt like people automatically assumed we were going to have a letdown. I don't think this group of guys is going to do something like that."

Ohio State's Chris Wells surges through the Spartans' defense. Wells rushed 12 times for 53 yards and a touchdown.
Dispatch photo by Renee Sauer

UP, UP AND AWAY

BY KEN GORDON

After its latest exhibition of power and glory, it's clear that Ohio State isn't competing against its opponents as much as it is measuring itself against perfection.

Consider that the No. 1 Buckeyes blew away Indiana like a house of straw, 44-3, improving their record to 8-0 (4-0 Big Ten) and extending the nation's longest win streak to 15.

And yet, the quarterback who threw for four touchdowns lamented a lost fumble. A kicker who just made a 51-yard field goal bemoaned his missed extra-point attempt.

> "I FEEL LIKE WE TOOK ONE MORE STEP, AND WE HAVE TO GET MUCH, MUCH BETTER."
>
> BUCKEYES COACH
> JIM TRESSEL

And the coach who oversees this destructive machine was still looking for more.

"I feel like we took one more step," Jim Tressel said, "and we have to get much, much better."

If they do, maybe opponents would be better served to forfeit than show up and risk injury.

Ohio State's Ted Ginn Jr. corrals a 31-yard touchdown pass from Troy Smith over Indiana's Tracy Porter early in the second quarter.
Dispatch photo by Neal C. Lauron

OCTOBER 21, 2006 • BUCKEYES 44, HOOSIERS 3

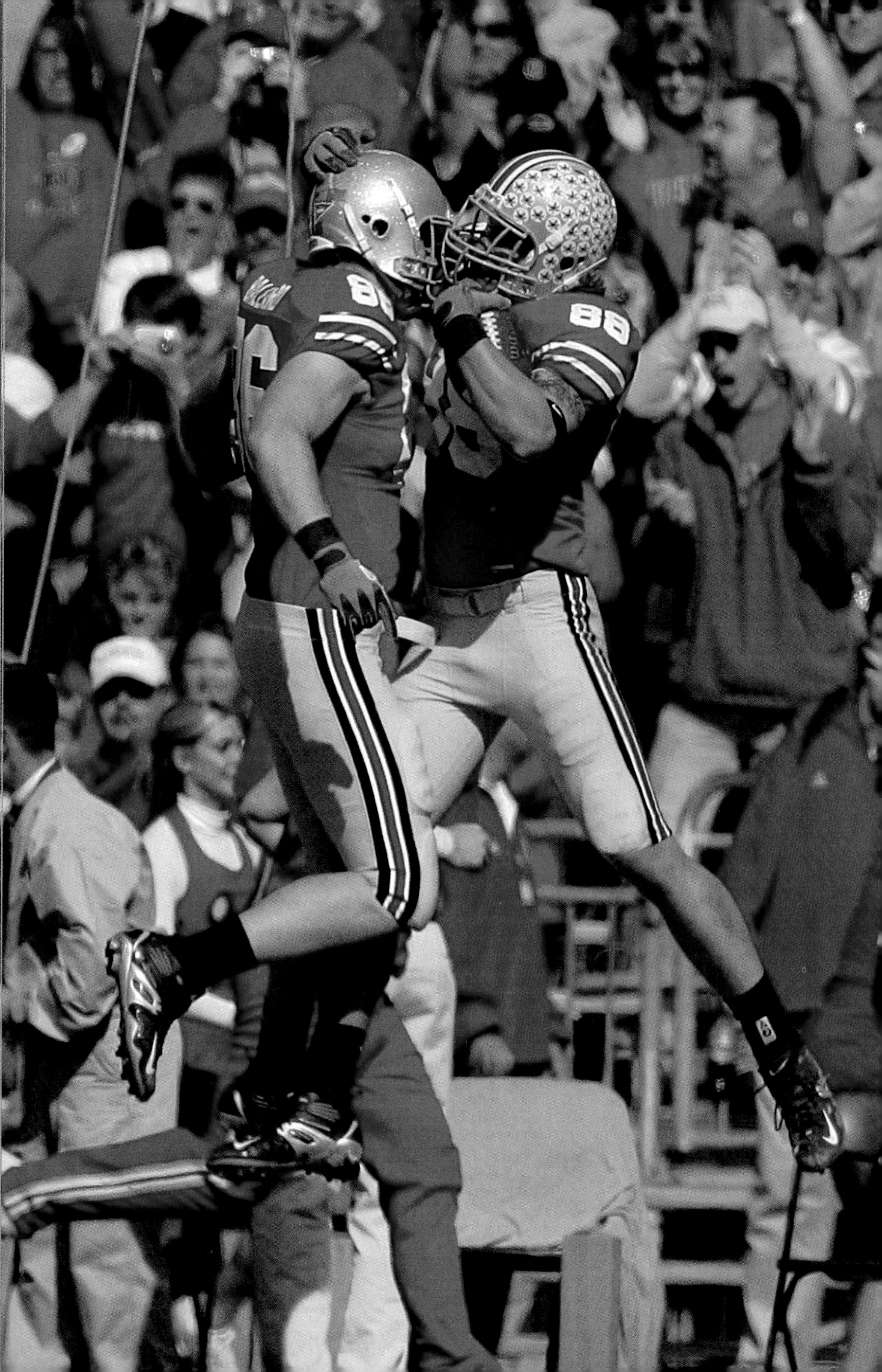

The Buckeyes rolled to a season-high 540 yards on offense. Quarterback Troy Smith matched his career high with four touchdown passes and provided yet another Heisman moment on one of those.

Three TDs were caught by tight ends, two by Rory Nicol, including one thrown by receiver Ted Ginn Jr. Running back Antonio Pittman had 105 yards rushing.

It was so bad that kicker Aaron Pettrey said he was tired after a day in which he kicked off six times and tried six extra points and a field goal.

"My legs, yeah, I'll get in the cold tub tomorrow," Pettrey said.

Defensively, the Buckeyes limited the Hoosiers (4-4, 2-2) to 165 yards, including 7 yards rushing. Cornerback Antonio Smith had a career day with 12 tackles, a sack and a forced fumble.

Quarterback Kellen Lewis threw for just 106 yards and was sacked four times, twice by Jay Richardson. Malcolm Jenkins and Andre Amos picked off passes from backup Blake Powers.

James Hardy, Indiana's dangerous 6-foot-7 receiver, was a non-factor (six catches, 45 yards).

"I am not going to be overly critical of any individual on our team," Hoosiers coach Terry Hoeppner said. "Ohio State took away a lot of things we wanted to do. We got outplayed by a team that on this day was a lot better than we were."

Rory Nicol (88) and teammate Jake Ballard (86) celebrate in the end zone after Nicol made a 23-yard TD reception in the first half. *Dispatch photo by Neal C. Lauron*

"MY THANKS TO OUR QUARTER-BACK—TROY JUST COMES OUT AND MAKES US GO, AND WE'RE LUCKY TO HAVE HIM."

BUCKEYES RECEIVER TED GINN JR.

And to think this all happened after the Buckeyes started slowly. Maybe knowing the game wasn't widely available on local television, Smith gave fans time to find their favorite watering hole and settle in before he set about executing Indiana, er, the game plan.

Ohio State went three-and-out on its first two possessions. Indiana took a 3-0 lead after Tracy Porter's 34-yard punt return set up the Hoosiers at the OSU 15-yard line.

Indiana gained exactly 0 yards in three plays, a defensive stand that boosted OSU's spirits.

"It was a critical situation where the defense was pushed back on the field, but we practice situations like that," cornerback Donald Washington said. "We try and prepare ourselves for the worst. We just tried to keep our composure."

From then on, Smith was simply shooting fish (Hoosiers) in a barrel (Ohio Stadium).

After misfiring on his first four passes, Smith threw three TDs in his next eight tosses.

The first came on a nice play-fake on third-and-1 to a wide-open Nicol. The second was one of his patented scrambling improvisational masterpieces.

Spinning away from Keith Burrus, Smith flung a pass off his back foot with Josh Bailey in his face. Ginn caught it for a 31-yard score that made it 14-3.

"My thanks to our quarterback," Ginn said. "Troy just comes out and makes us go, and we're lucky to have him."

Maurice Wells (34) makes a long gain in the second half. Wells had nine carries for 62 yards against the Hoosiers.
Dispatch photo by Jeff Hinckley

	1st	2nd	3rd	4th	Final
Indiana	**3**	**0**	**0**	**0**	**3**
Ohio State	**7**	**21**	**10**	**6**	**44**

Scoring Summary

1st—

IND Starr 34-yard field goal—4 plays, 0 yards in 1:08.

OSU Nicol 23-yard pass from Smith (Pettrey kick)—7 plays, 87 yards in 1:57.

2nd—

OSU Ginn Jr. 31-yard pass from Smith (Pettrey kick)—4 plays, 53 yards in 1:35.

OSU Gonzalez 5-yard pass from Smith (Pettrey kick)—9 plays, 78 yards in 3:59.

OSU Ballard 1-yard pass from Smith (Pettrey kick)—3 plays, 49 yards in 0:31.

3rd—

OSU Nicol 38-yard pass from Ginn Jr. (Pettrey kick)—3 plays, 58 yards in 1:03.

OSU Pettrey 51-yard field goal—6 plays, 47 yards in 3:34.

4th—

OSU C. Wells 12-yard run (Pettrey kick failed)—9 plays, 68 yards in 4:46.

Team Statistics

	IND	OSU
First Downs	16	25
Rushes-Yards (Net)	28-7	39-270
Passing Yards (Net)	158	270
Passes Comp-Att-Int	20-35-2	17-25-0
Total Offense Plays-Yards	63-165	64-540
Fumbles Returns-Yards	0-0	0-0
Punt Returns-Yards	2-40	4-42
Kickoff Returns-Yards	6-94	2-29
Interception Returns-Yards	0-0	2-7
Punts (Number-Avg)	8-42.6	3-42.3
Fumbles-Lost	3-0	1-1
Sacks By (Number-Yards)	0-0	4-46
Penalties-Yards	5-30	4-40
Possession Time	30:47	29:13

Leading 21-3, Ohio State got the ball back at midfield with 51 seconds left in the half. Tressel went for it, and Smith complied, completing three straight throws for a TD and a 25-point halftime lead.

Asked about the aggressive play-calling, Tressel cited Indiana's three comeback victories this season, the most dramatic after a 25-7 deficit.

"So what should make you think you shouldn't get as many points as you can to win?" he said.

Ginn made that moot shortly after halftime. Last week at Michigan State, a Ginn pass was called, but the play broke down and he threw incomplete toward Nicol.

This week, it was designed for Nicol. Smith pitched to Ginn rolling right. Ginn threw it, and Indiana linebacker Adam McClurg fell down, leaving Nicol wide open. He gathered it in and completed the 38-yard score.

That made it 35-3.

"Special people in special places, they do special things," Smith said.

He was referring to Ginn, but against Indiana, that applied to a number of Buckeyes.

Ohio State's Larry Grant (6) and Antonio Smith (14) stop Indiana's Kellen Lewis in the second half. The Buckeyes' defense held the Hoosiers to seven total rushing yards. *Dispatch photo by Neal C. Lauron*

0-FER FOR GOPHERS

BY KEN GORDON

Their work appeared to be finished, the hay safely in the barn with Ohio State leading 37-0 early in the fourth quarter.

OSU's defensive starters went to the sideline and the back-ups came in to play out the string.

But then the Buckeyes fumbled a punt back to Minnesota, giving the Gophers the ball at the Ohio State 36-yard line.

The Buckeyes had come close to posting a shutout several times this season, and they wanted one badly. The starters prevailed upon defensive coordinator Jim Heacock to go back in.

He complied.

> "THAT'S ALWAYS A BIG MOTIVATING FACTOR. EVERYBODY HAS A GOOD TIME KNOWING WE PUT A GOOSE EGG UP THERE."
>
> BUCKEYES DEFENSIVE END JAY RICHARDSON

"Did we (put the starters back in)? Yeah, we probably did." Heacock said, a bit sheepishly. "(The shutout) was a goal of these kids, and, I mean, give them an opportunity. It's what you shoot for."

The defense responded. Minnesota reached the 15 and faced a fourth-and-1. Quarterback Bryan Cupito was stuffed for no gain,

Lawrence Wilson (87) jumps over Minnesota quarterback Bryan Cupito on his way to congratulate teammate James Laurinaitis (33) after Laurinaitis sacked Cupito.
Dispatch photo by Neal C. Lauron

Ohio State's Malcolm Jenkins (2) turns upfield after intercepting a pass intended for Minnesota's Jack Simmons (80) in the first half. The Buckeyes had three interceptions during the game. *Dispatch photo by Neal C. Lauron*

and the Buckeyes defenders ran off the field jumping for joy.

They got their shutout, 44-0, the first since a 20-0 whitewashing of Northwestern in 2003.

"That's always a big motivating factor," defensive end Jay Richardson said of the shutout. "Everybody has a good time knowing we put a goose egg up there."

The shutout was the one statistic that made this game stand out from a string of mind-numbingly similar Ohio State victories this season.

The Buckeyes (9-0, 5-0 Big Ten) extended their win streak to 16, longest in the nation. Their average score this season has been 36-7.

This win was preceded by a 44-3 trouncing of Indiana and a 37-7 win at Michigan State in which the backups gave up a touchdown in the final two minutes.

OSU outgained Minnesota 484-182, including a 266-47 edge in rushing yards. Four different Buckeyes players rushed for touchdowns, led by Antonio Pittman (116 yards, two TDs).

On a windy, cold day, quarterback Troy Smith didn't post huge numbers (14 of 21 passing, 183 yards), but he threw for one TD and rushed for 43 yards and another score.

Eight different receivers caught passes.

The Buckeyes lost three fumbles, a shocking total considering they had just six turnovers all season coming in. But three interceptions of Cupito (15 of 23, 120 yards) balanced the ledger.

The Gophers (3-6, 0-5) have lost five of their past six games.

"Today we faced an incredible football team," Minnesota coach Glen Mason said. "We have had many problems, and we continue to have problems."

OSU's defense was tested early with the score 10-0. Smith lost a fumble and Minnesota faced fourth-and-1 at the Ohio State 19. Richardson penetrated and tripped up Amir Pinnix, and safety Jamario O'Neal finished him off for no gain.

"Emotionally, any time you stop someone on short yardage, there's an effect," OSU coach Jim Tressel said. "I'm sure that took a little emotion from the Golden Gophers."

Antonio Pittman fights for extra yardage against a horde of Minnesota defenders. *Dispatch photo by Eric Albrecht*

OCTOBER 28, 2006 • BUCKEYES 44, GOPHERS 0

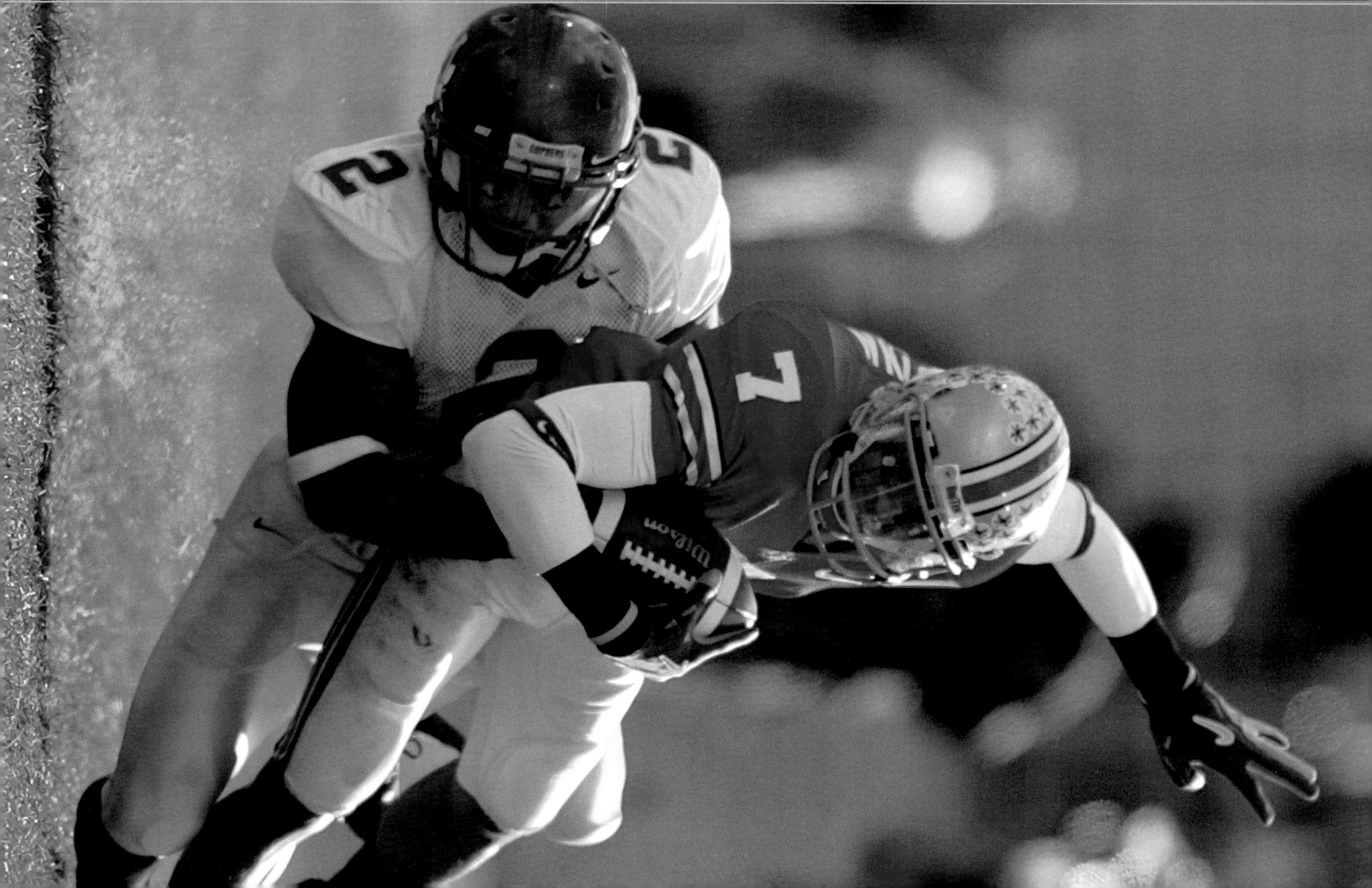

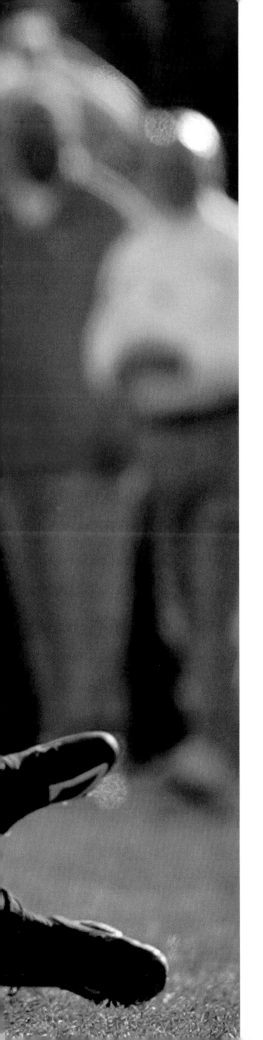

The Buckeyes responded with a 10-play, 71-yard drive capped by a Smith scoring toss on a perfect fade pattern to Brian Robiskie. The lead was 17-0 at the half.

Any doubts about the outcome were erased when OSU converted third-quarter interceptions by Antonio Smith and O'Neal into touchdowns for a 30-0 lead.

The Buckeyes now have forced 20 turnovers this season and scored 86 points off them. Their opponents have forced nine turnovers and not yet converted them to any points.

"We're getting better," Tressel said. "We understand we have more tests to go, but you have to feel good about the progress."

OSU's defense missed tackle Quinn Pitcock because of a concussion suffered last week, but welcomed back tackle David Patterson, who had missed two games after arthroscopic knee surgery. But its performance was redemption for last year's Minnesota game, in which the Buckeyes surrendered 396 passing yards and 587 overall, second-most in school history.

"They put up so many yards on us last year, to come out here and shut them down like we did, it's kind of a pride thing," said cornerback Malcolm Jenkins, who recorded his fourth interception of the season. He also pointed out the obvious, that posting a shutout "almost guarantees a win. ... We're very excited and happy about it, and we'll keep trying to get some more."

Ted Ginn Jr. is brought down by Minnesota's Dominic Jones in the first quarter. *Dispatch photo by Fred Squillante*

	1st	2nd	3rd	4th	Final
Minnesota	0	0	0	0	**0**
Ohio State	10	7	13	14	**44**

Scoring Summary

1st—
OSU Pittman 10-yard run (Pettrey kick)—8 plays, 57 yards in 4:01.

OSU Pettrey 42-yard field goal—7 plays, 48 yards in 3:09.

2nd—
OSU Robiskie 18-yard pass from Smith (Pettrey kick)—10 plays, 71 yards in 4:07.

3rd—
OSU Smith 21-yard run (Pettrey kick)—3 plays, 23 yards in 1:11.

OSU Pittman 13-yard run (Pettrey kick blocked)—5 plays, 41 yards in 2:09.

4th—
OSU C. Wells 3-yard run (Pettrey kick)—10 plays, 74 yards in 4:55.

OSU Zwick 1-yard run (Pettrey kick)—14 plays, 85 yards in 6:44.

Team Statistics

	MINN	OSU
First Downs	10	29
Rushes-Yards (Net)	26-47	46-266
Passing Yards (Net)	135	218
Passes Comp-Att-Int	15-28-3	17-25-0
Total Offense Plays-Yards	54-182	71-484
Fumble Returns-Yards	0-0	0-0
Punt Returns-Yards	0-0	3-17
Kickoff Returns-Yards	3-58	1-35
Interception Returns-Yards	0-0	3-37
Punts (Number-Avg)	5-37.2	0-0.0
Fumbles-Lost	1-0	4-3
Sacks By (Number-Yards)	1-6	2-10
Penalties-Yards	4-20	3-40
Possession Time	27:19	32:41

Antonio Pittman gains yardage against Minnesota's Mario Reese (48) and Jamal Harris (15) on Ohio State's first possession. Pittman finished the game with two touchdowns on 21 carries and 117 yards. *Dispatch photo by Fred Squillante*

NO FUN FOR NO. 1

BY KEN GORDON

Fewer than two minutes remained and thousands of orange-clad Illinois fans were jumping and yelling in Memorial Stadium. A loud chorus of "I-L-L" and "I-N-I" echoed across the field in the chilly evening air.

The band played, a bell tolled.

The Illini trailed by just seven points and were lining up for an onside kick.

This had not happened to Ohio State in a while, certainly not in this charmed season, when the Buckeyes had rolled nine opponents by an average of 29 points.

Illinois was not a meek and mild

> "WE KNEW THIS WAS THEIR ONE AND ONLY CHANCE TO HAVE A LITTLE BIT OF GLORY, TO KNOCK OFF OHIO STATE. WE KNEW THEY WEREN'T JUST GOING TO ROLL OVER FOR US."
>
> BUCKEYES DEFENSIVE END
> JAY RICHARDSON

2-7 team. This was a hard-hitting, enthusiastic group that was making the nation's No. 1 team sweat.

Jay Richardson (99) and Malcolm Jenkins (2) congratulate teammate James Laurinaitis (33) after Laurinaitis intercepted a pass from Illinois QB Tim Brasic in the fourth quarter. *Dispatch photo by Neal C. Lauron*

Ted Ginn Jr. eludes the tackle of Illinios defender J Leman. Ginn Jr. had five catches for 22 yards against the Illini.
Dispatch photo by Mike Munden

The kick fluttered through the hands of Ohio State safety Brandon Mitchell and wiggled around for a few tense moments before receiver Brian Robiskie fell on it.

With 1:36 left, Ohio State ran all but four seconds off the clock and held on for a 17-10 victory.

"I really thought we were going to get it," Illinois coach Ron Zook said of the kickoff. "But it wasn't meant to be."

This, finally, was the test Ohio State (10-0, 6-0) figured it would get at some point this season. Most expected it would come from Texas or Penn State in September.

But after trailing 17-0 at halftime, the Illini (2-8, 1-5) cracked down on defense, giving up just 29 second-half yards and scoring 10 fourth-quarter points to suddenly make it a squeaker.

Ohio State's Brian Robiskie gets upended by Justin Harrison in the first half. Robiskie had two receptions for 33 yards.
Dispatch photo by Chris Russell

"We knew this was their one and only chance to have a little bit of glory, to knock off Ohio State," defensive end Jay Richardson said. "We knew they weren't just going to roll over for us."

Illinois ended up outgaining OSU overall, 233 yards to 224. By seven points, it was the fewest points the Buckeyes scored this season and the narrowest margin of victory.

Quarterback Troy Smith failed to throw a touchdown pass for the first time in 12 games, passing for just 108 yards with an interception. Running back Antonio Pittman was stuffed for 58 yards on 32 carries, with 20 carries of 2 or fewer yards.

"They came out here and gave us all they had," Pittman said.

freshman quarterback Juice Williams earlier, but after backup Tim Brasic threw two incompletions, Williams came on to fire a 24-yard pass to Columbus native Jeff Cumberland, jump-starting the drive.

Three plays later, a wicked Laurinaitis knocked Williams back out and sent him for X-rays to check for a broken jaw. Brasic helped the Illini finish off a 10-play, 80-yard march for the score that made it 17-10.

After the onside kick, Illinois used its last two timeouts on Pittman runs. After a third run, the clock drained to 18 seconds before Ohio State punted down to the Illini 2 with four ticks left.

> "A WIN IS A WIN, ANY WHICH WAY YOU CUT IT. WHETHER YOU SCORE 50 POINTS OR YOU SCORE 17, WHO CARES? WE WON TODAY AND WE'LL CONTINUE TO GROW. THERE'S GOING TO BE CRITICS, THERE'S GOING TO BE NAYSAYERS, ANY WHICH WAY YOU DO IT."
>
> BUCKEYES QUARTERBACK
> TROY SMITH

A desperation pass and a series of laterals petered out at the Illinois 19, and OSU won.

The Buckeyes played it cool afterward. There were dual spins coming from the locker room: One was a bit of defiance, from Smith.

"A win is a win, any which way you cut it. Whether you score 50 points or you score 17," he said, "who cares? We won today and we'll continue to grow. There's going to be critics, there's going to be naysayers, any which way you do it."

Even with a lethargic offense, Ohio State was in control until the final minutes. Leading 17-3, Smith was picked off, but Buckeyes linebacker James Laurinaitis responded with a pick to apparently seal the victory with 4:50 left in the game.

The Illini forced a quick punt and took over at its 20-yard line with 3:43 left. They had benched

	1st	2nd	3rd	4th	Final
Ohio State	**7**	**10**	**0**	**0**	**17**
Illinois	**0**	**0**	**0**	**10**	**10**

Scoring Summary

1st—

OSU C. Wells 2-yard run (Pettrey kick)—14 plays, 80 yards in 6:44.

2nd—

OSU Pittman 1-yard run (Pettrey kick)—8 plays, 38 yards in 4:24.

OSU Pettrey 50-yard field goal—11 plays, 40 yards in 5:16.

4th—

ILL Reda 27-yard field goal—7 plays, 37 yards in 2:29.

ILL Mendenhall 3-yard run (Reda kick)—10 plays, 80 yards in 2:03.

	OSU	ILL
First Downs	17	13
Rushes-Yards (Net)	47-116	22-99
Passing Yards (Net)	108	134
Passes Comp-Att-Int	13-23-1	14-35-1
Total Offense Plays-Yards	70-224	57-233
Fumble Returns-Yards	0-0	0-0
Punt Returns-Yards	3-28	0-0
Kickoff Returns-Yards	1-14	2-24
Interception Returns-Yards	1-5	1-0
Punts (Number-Avg)	7-40.7	7-38.9
Fumbles-Lost	3-1	2-1
Sacks By (Number-Yards)	0-0	3-23
Penalties-Yards	5-39	1-15
Possession Time	36:17	23:43

"IN LIFE OR IN FOOTBALL, YOU LEARN MORE IN YOUR SUFFERING THAN YOU DO IN YOUR WONDERFUL MOMENTS, SO I THINK WE'LL LEARN SOMETHING."

BUCKEYES COACH
JIM TRESSEL

But the other theme was that OSU needed a tough game, that the succession of ho-hum victories had begun to turn the Buckeyes soft inside.

"I think it's a good thing for us, it's humbling," cornerback Malcolm Jenkins said. "We come out (on) cloud nine, we're back to reality. We know we can be beat."

So why did they need humbling? Had they felt invincible?

"We kind of got away from the grind period," Jenkins said. "Getting on our grind and knowing we have to go every week as hard as anybody else."

Coach Jim Tressel mixed equal parts of crediting the Illini and realizing that a close call could be a teaching tool.

A close call that ends in a win, that is.

"I think every time you're tested and every time you're bruised and battered and so forth, I think it's always good for you," Tressel said. "In life or in football, you learn more in your suffering than you do in your wonderful moments, so I think we'll learn something."

James Laurinaitis hammers Illinois quarterback Isiah Williams in the second half. The Illini had no passing touchdowns.
Dispatch photo by Neal C. Lauron

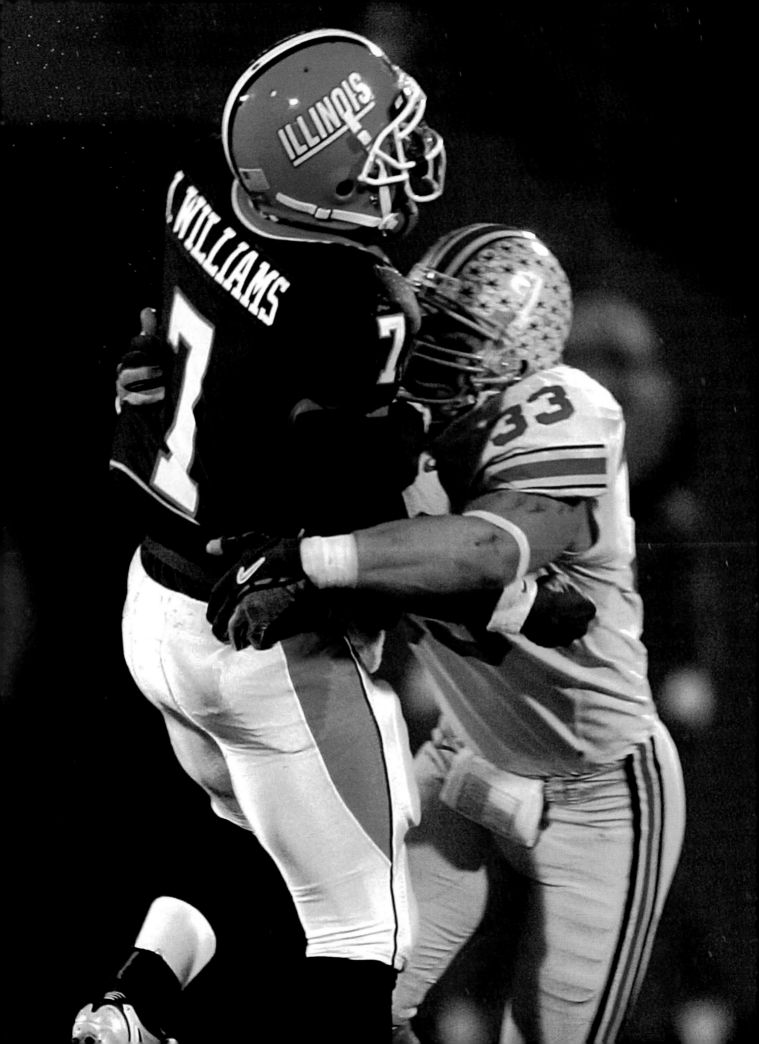

11 AND 0; BIG ONE TO GO

BY KEN GORDON

Northwestern managed a neat trick: The Wildcats gave Ohio State a game while also giving OSU the game.

The Wildcats moved the ball well on the Buckeyes, but they also committed five turnovers and had a punt blocked.

Coming off a shaky win last week at Illinois, the Buckeyes thanked the Wildcats very much, converting all six mistakes into points and winning 54-10.

The result for the top-ranked Buckeyes was a good, stiff workout but also a much-needed shot of confidence as they head into their winner-take-all showdown next week against No. 2 Michigan.

> "OUR GUYS KEEP COMING, AND WE ALWAYS TALK ABOUT THAT YOU BETTER HAVE A RELENTLESS DEFENSE ... AND THAT'S THE WAY OUR DEFENSE IS."
>
> BUCKEYES COACH
> JIM TRESSEL

Brandon Mitchell (32) is hoisted up by David Patterson after Mitchell's 47-yard interception return TD against Northwestern.
Dispatch photo by Mike Munden

NOVEMBER 11, 2006 • BUCKEYES 54, WILDCATS 10

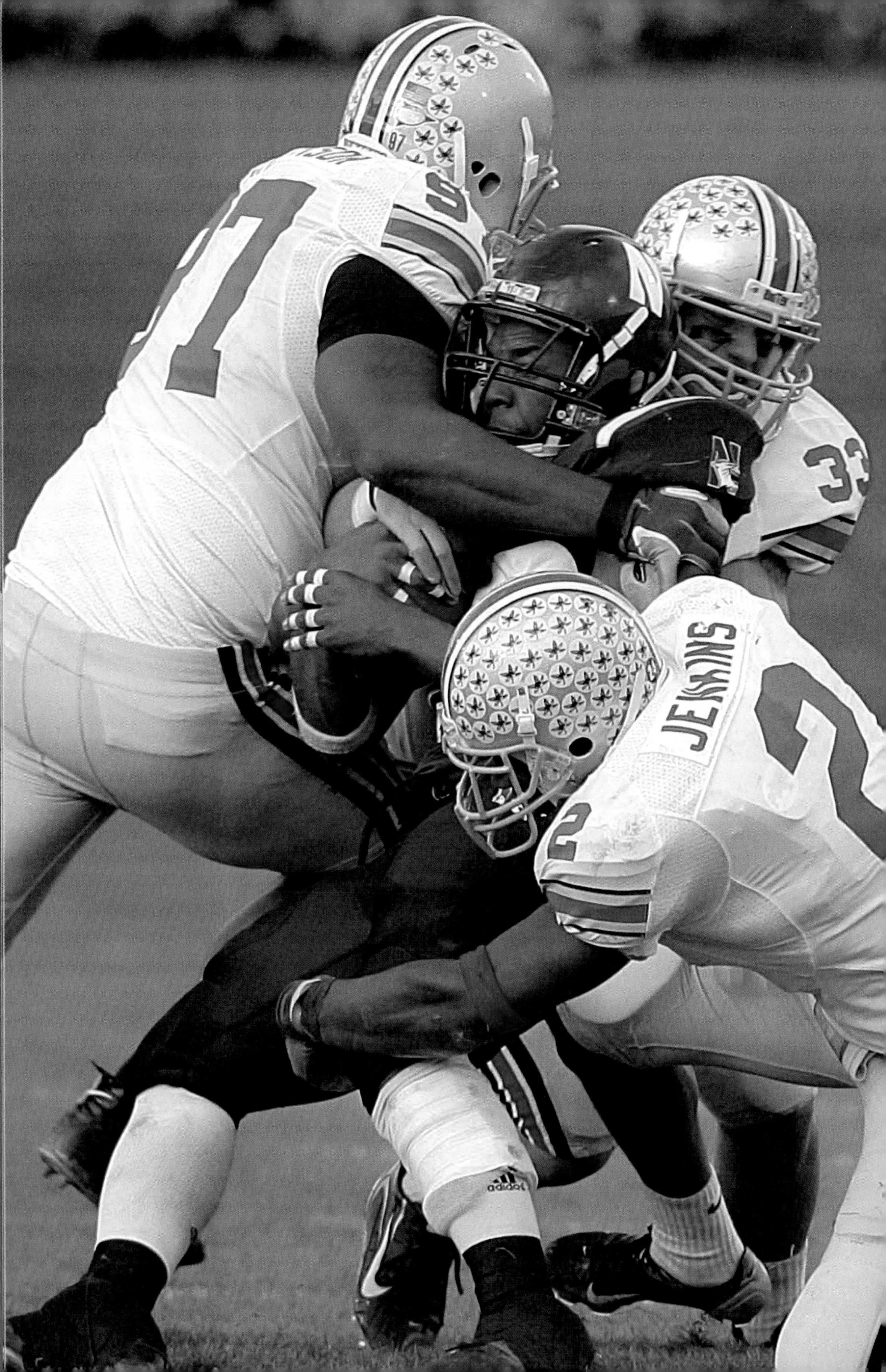

"You can't have two games like that in a row and expect to go into a game like next week in that type of shape," tailback Antonio Pittman said of a 17-10 win at Illinois in which OSU went to the ground in the second half.

The point total was the Buckeyes' highest since a 72-0 victory over Pittsburgh on Sept. 21, 1996.

Troy Smith threw for 184 yards and four touchdowns, tying his career high. Two scores were to Brian Hartline, and one each went to Ted Ginn Jr. and Anthony Gonzalez.

Pittman went over 1,000 yards rushing for the season with 80 yards and a touchdown, and freshman back Chris "Beanie" Wells atoned for his recent fumbling problems with a mistake-free day (99 yards, TD).

It was impressive, considering the offensive line played a second straight game without left tackle Alex Boone (knee). Tim Schafer and Jim Cordle rotated at the spot.

"This was a good game after the game that happened last week," center Doug Datish said. "It was good to kind of answer some questions and get things rolling and get a better vibe."

But this wasn't a case of Ohio State (11-0, 7-0) simply returning to its regularly scheduled blowout. The Wildcats (3-8, 1-6) made the Buckeyes sweat a bit.

David Patterson (97), James Laurinaitis (33), and Malcolm Jenkins (2) team up to stop Northwestern's Tyrell Sutton in the first half. *Dispatch photo by Neal C. Lauron*

"OUR DEFENSE DOES A GREAT JOB OF PUTTING PRESSURE ON. OUR GUYS KEEP COMING, AND WE ALWAYS TALK ABOUT THAT YOU BETTER HAVE A RELENTLESS DEFENSE ... AND THAT'S THE WAY OUR DEFENSE IS."

BUCKEYES COACH
JIM TRESSEL

Northwestern outgained Ohio State in the first half, 235 yards to 229.

Behind sophomore quarterback C.J. Bacher (17-of-28 passing, 212 yards), the Wildcats put together some impressive drives, including 69 yards for a field goal and 75 yards for a touchdown.

The problem was, that made the score just 27-10 late in the first half because the Wildcats spent the rest of the half messing up.

Northwestern turned the ball over twice on its first five plays and three times on its first 14 snaps—two fumbles and an interception. The pick by Brandon Mitchell was returned 46 yards for a score and a 21-0 lead by the end of the first quarter.

"We moved the ball well in the first half, but you have to respect the ball," Wildcats coach Pat Fitzgerald said. "You cannot gift-wrap it like that for them. Christmas isn't for a month and a half yet, but Merry Christmas."

But Smith gave the Wildcats a present as well, tossing up a long pass intended for Ginn that Sherrick McManis intercepted.

"Probably a poor call, asking him to throw a home run into the wind," Ohio State coach Jim Tressel said.

No worries. Bacher fumbled it right back to the Buckeyes, and Smith then unleashed his weekly Heisman Trophy moment.

On third-and-20 from the Wildcats' 34-yard line, Smith stood in against a fierce blitz, got

OSU head coach Jim Tressel and the Buckeyes have their game faces on just before the game with Northwestern.
Dispatch photo by Mike Munden

	1st	2nd	3rd	4th	Final
Ohio State	21	12	14	7	54
Northwestern	0	10	0	0	10

Scoring Summary

1st—

OSU Hartline 14-yard pass from Smith (Pettrey kick)—5 plays, 55 yards in 2:09.

OSU Pittman 1-yard run (Pettrey kick)—4 plays, 27 yards in 1:24.

OSU Mitchell 46-yard interception return (Pettrey kick).

2nd—

NU Howells 29-yard field goal—12 plays, 69 yards in 4:39.

OSU Hartline 9-yard pass from Smith (Pettrey kick blocked)—3 plays, 16 yards in 1:33.

NU Sutton 8-yard pass from Bacher (Howells kick)—6 plays, 75 yards in 2:25.

OSU Ginn Jr. 34-yard pass from Smith (Trapasso rush failed)—3 plays, 24 yards in 0:29.

3rd—

OSU Gonzalez 6-yard pass from Smith (Pettrey kick)—5 plays, 39 yards in 2:10.

OSU C. Wells 1-yard run (Pettrey kick)—9 plays, 80 yards in 5:21.

4th—

OSU Boeckman 4-yard run (Pretorius kick)—8 plays, 42 yards in 3:53.

Team Statistics

	OSU	NU
First Downs	22	17
Rushes-Yards (Net)	44-231	24-68
Passing Yards (Net)	194	229
Passes Comp-Att-Int	14-24-1	21-36-2
Total Offense Plays-Yards	68-425	60-297
Fumble Returns-Yards	0-0	0-0
Punt Returns-Yards	2-9	1-21
Kickoff Returns-Yards	3-82	4-56
Interception Returns-Yards	2-51	1-0
Punts (Number-Avg)	2-38.5	4-25.2
Fumbles-Lost	1-1	3-3
Sacks By (Number-Yards)	3-14	1-9
Penalties-Yards	3-30	2-17
Possession Time	31:52	26:27

popped as he threw, yet feathered a perfect pass into the hands of a tightly covered Ginn down the left sideline.

It was 33-10 at the half, and Northwestern finally was subdued.

"Ted made a great play on the ball," Smith said. "What more can you ask for from a guy who's fighting off a defender (McManis) and he's making plays?"

The Buckeyes finished off the Wildcats after halftime. An interception by Ross Homan ended Bacher's day early in the third quarter.

Wells had a 33-yard rumble and capped the drive with a score that made it 47-10. Third-string quarterback Todd Boeckman ran in for the final TD.

The most telling final statistic was 127-0—as in, OSU now has scored 127 points off its opponents' turnovers to zero points against the Buckeyes after their miscues.

"Our defense does a great job of putting pressure on," Tressel said. "Our guys keep coming, and we always talk about that you better have a relentless defense ... and that's the way our defense is."

Most important to Tressel, his crew got back on track after the speed bump in Champaign. Just in time, too.

"It was good to get a decisive win," Tressel said. "When you have a rivalry like (Ohio State-Michigan), you're hoping you're playing your best football in the last game, and I think we've progressed."

An Ohio State fan is ready for The Game against Michigan. *Dispatch photo by Mike Munden*

BO-WOODY KINSHIP SURVIVED RIVALRY

BY BOB HUNTER

Bo Schembechler's death on Friday, November 17, 2006, was accompanied by more than a pinch of irony.

In life, Schembechler helped shove the Ohio State-Michigan rivalry into the sports stratosphere, engaging in a "10-year war" with old boss Woody Hayes that seemed to transform it into more than just a game.

> "I COACHED FOR WOODY WHEN WOODY WAS REALLY WOODY. ... I WOULDN'T CHANGE THAT EXPERIENCE FOR ANYTHING IN THE WORLD BECAUSE I LEARNED A LOT."
>
> BO SCHEMBECHLER

In death, the day before what some are calling the biggest Ohio State-Michigan game ever, he gave it back some perspective. The sudden loss of the former Michigan head coach to heart failure at least temporarily interrupted the frenzy created by the most-hyped game in the series' rich history.

Ohio State head coach Woody Hayes greets Michigan head coach Bo Schembechler before the start of one of their legendary matchups.
Photo by Chance Brockway

He had tried to do that during game week while he was still alive. Schembechler opened a news conference in Ann Arbor by talking about the death of former Wolverines quarterback Tom Slade the night before. His words offered a perspective that his own death would accentuate four days later.

"I was thinking about this game with two great undefeated teams playing against each other," Schembechler said. "And last night we lost Tom Slade ... so there are some things that are more important than this game on Saturday."

Despite all the bluster and bravado that followed these two cranky characters through the 1970s, Schembechler and Hayes were never the acrimonious enemies they appeared to be. Bo was a graduate assistant coach on Woody's first Ohio State staff in 1951, and after a stint in the Army and jobs at three other schools he returned to Hayes' staff for five more years.

"I escaped from Columbus when I got the head-coaching job at Miami (University)," Schembechler said this week. "But I had a wonderful experience there because I coached for Woody when Woody was really Woody. He was the most irascible guy that ever lived and the worst guy in the world to work for. But I wouldn't change that experi-

ence for anything in the world because ... I learned a lot."

> "WHEN WOODY DIED, IT WAS SUCH AN EMOTIONAL ROLLER COASTER FOR [BO], WE TOOK TWO DAYS OFF OF SPRING DRILLS TO HONOR WOODY."
>
> FORMER MICHIGAN DEFENSIVE BACK DAVID KEY

He landed the job at Michigan at precisely the time when he could do the most damage to Hayes' Buckeyes. With a star-studded sophomore class, the Buckeyes had won the national championship in 1968, closing out the regular season with a 50-14 win over Bump Elliott's Wolverines.

It set up another national championship run in 1969, and the No. 1 Buckeyes were on the way until Schembechler's Wolverines pulled a stunning 24-12 upset. It started an escalation in the rivalry that has continued to this day.

Although this game might be the biggest in terms of rankings and prestige, the 1970 revenge game was probably more important to Ohio State players and fans than any in school history. The Buckeyes won 20-9, setting the stage for eight more years of Woody-Bo battles.

Ohio State fans hated Bo and Michigan fans hated Woody, so it was natural to assume the two men hated each other. Later, when Woody was retired and Bo's coaching career was winding down, we learned that the image of "hatred" masked an enormous respect.

"Several times (Schembechler) would be sick or ill and he would never ever miss a

Bo Schembechler (left) was a graduate assistant coach and later an assistant coach on Woody Hayes' staff before he took the reins at Michigan. *Photo by Chance Brockway*

practice," former Michigan defensive back David Key said. "Once he had kidney stones and I swear he passed the kidney stones in the middle of practice just so he wouldn't miss it. But when Woody died, it was such an emotional roller coaster for him, we took two days off of spring drills to honor Woody."

Woody felt the same way about Schembechler. In 1987, he heard Bo was speaking at a luncheon in Dayton. Even though he was in poor health, Woody asked a friend to drive him over there just so he could introduce Schembechler. Bo later remem-

bered how feeble Woody looked leaning on his cane but said he gave a 20-minute introduction and then stayed for every word of his old friend's speech.

Woody died the next day.

DASH TO THE DESERT

BY KEN GORDON

What was a tunnel of pride on the way out became a tunnel of triumph on the way back.

Before their game with Michigan, Ohio State players ran through the traditional "tunnel of pride," a double line of former players who gather for the last home game of every season.

Moments after their 42-39 victory over Michigan, the Buckeyes fought their way through the frenzy of fans who swirled around the Ohio Stadium field.

As players trotted up the tunnel to the locker room, people pawed at their uniforms, held up cell phones to take pictures and screamed in joy.

Just inside the tunnel, receiver Ted Ginn Jr. did a pull-up on an overhead bar, trying to see above the crowd and find a teammate in the din.

They wanted to be together to enjoy this moment that meant so much:

It was a win over their archrivals, their fifth in six years. An outright Big Ten championship, Ohio State's first since 1984.

A trip to the national championship game in Glendale, Arizona, their second in five years.

A successful defense of their No. 1 ranking against a No. 2 team, the second time this season they did it.

Chris Wells (28) breaks free for a 52-yard touchdown run against Michigan. Wells carried the ball five times for 60 yards. *Dispatch photo by Mike Munden*

MIchigan QB Chad Henne is brought down by James Laurinaitis (33) and Antonio Smith (14). *Dispatch photo by Mike Munden*

Brian Robiskie makes a reception and flips after getting hit by Michigan's Morgan Trent in the first half. Robiskie pulled in seven catches for 89 yards and a touchdown against the Wolverines. *Dispatch photo by Neal C. Lauron*

The Buckeyes are 12-0 and finished 8-0 in the Big Ten. They extended their win streak to 19, longest in the country.

Quarterback Troy Smith said he was at a loss for words, but what he said next was as eloquent as anything else he has ever said.

"The feeling is unparalleled," he said, with a silly, dazed grin. "You wouldn't be able to understand it unless you ran the gassers we ran, ran the hills we ran, pushed the sleds. When that heat and sun is beating down on your back in the summer, the commitment and the focus.

"Words can't express what I feel right now. I'll probably be wearing my smile for the rest of this week. I love every single one of my teammates with the deepest passion you can possibly have for another person."

It was a shocking offensive explosion, as both teams shredded heretofore vaunted defenses.

The teams combined for 81 points and 890 yards against units that came in ranked No. 1 in the nation in scoring (Ohio State at 7.8 points per game) and No. 1 against the run (Michigan at 29.9).

Ohio State racked up 503 yards, including 187 rushing.

"I never expected that to happen," Wolverines defensive end LaMarr Woodley said.

Ohio State's Antonio Pittman celebrates with the crowd after the Buckeyes beat Michigan 42-39. Pittman carried the ball 18 times for 140 yards and a touchdown. *Dispatch photo by Lisa Marie Miller*

An Ohio State fan celebrates as her Buckeyes are victorious over the Wolverines. *Dispatch photo by Chris Russell*

Smith likely locked up the Heisman Trophy with a 316-yard, four-touchdown performance. It was his third career 300-yard game, two of which have come against the Wolverines. He is 25-2 as a starter (15-0 at home) and broke the school record for TD passes in a season with 30.

"I would think he clinched the Heisman; I don't think there'd be any question about that," said coach Jim Tressel, who improved to 5-1 against Michigan.

Smith's four TDs went to four receivers. Ginn Jr. caught eight passes for 104 yards. Running backs Antonio Pittman (139 yards) and Chris "Beanie" Wells each had scoring runs of 50-plus yards.

But the Wolverines (11-1, 7-1) did not go quietly. Though the program was rocked by the death of former coach Bo Schembechler just a day earlier, coach Lloyd Carr said he did not use that as motivation, saying it wouldn't be fair to Schembechler.

"WORDS CAN'T EXPRESS WHAT I FEEL RIGHT NOW. I'LL PROBABLY BE WEARING MY SMILE FOR THE REST OF THIS WEEK. I LOVE EVERY SINGLE ONE OF MY TEAMMATES WITH THE DEEPEST PASSION YOU CAN POSSIBLY HAVE FOR ANOTHER PERSON."

BUCKEYES QUARTERBACK
TROY SMITH

Trailing 28-14 at halftime, though, it certainly looked as if they drew some sort of inspiration in the locker room.

Taking advantage of two of Ohio State's uncharacteristic three turnovers, Michigan drew to 28-24 midway through the third quarter and then 35-31 early in the fourth.

Running back Mike Hart rushed for 142 yards and three TDs.

"Their defense played good, but they're not as good as people thought," Hart said. "There's nothing special about that defense."

Ted Ginn Jr. implores the crowd to make more noise in the final seconds of the game. *Dispatch photo by Chris Russell*

	1st	2nd	3rd	4th	Final
Michigan	7	7	10	15	39
Ohio State	7	21	7	7	42

Scoring Summary

1st—

MICH Hart 1-yard run (Rivas kick)—7 plays, 80 yards in 2:28.

OSU Hall 1-yard pass from Smith (Pettrey kick)—14 plays, 69 yards in 6:10.

2nd—

OSU C. Wells 52-yard run (Pettrey kick)—2 plays, 58 yards in 0:57.

OSU Ginn Jr. 39-yard pass from Smith (Pettrey kick)—4 plays, 91 yards in 1:44.

MICH Arrington 37-yard pass from Henne (Rivas kick)—6 plays, 80 yards in 3:27.

OSU Gonzalez 8-yard pass from Smith (Pettrey kick)—9 plays, 80 yards in 2:08.

3rd—

MICH Hart 2-yard run (Rivas kick)—5 plays, 60 yards in 1:59.

MICH Rivas 39-yard field goal—4 plays, 3 yards in 2:07.

OSU Pittman 56-yard run (Pettrey kick)—2 plays, 65 yards in 0:37.

4th—

MICH Hart 1-yard run (Rivas kick)—3 plays, 9 yards in 0:40.

OSU Robiskie 13-yard pass from Smith (Pettrey kick)—11 plays, 83 yards in 5:00.

MICH Ecker 16-yard pass from Henne (Breaston pass from Henne)—11 plays, 81 yards in 3:11.

Team Statistics

	MICH	OSU
First Downs	17	24
Rushes-Yards (Net)	30-130	29-187
Passing Yards (Net)	267	316
Passes Comp-Att-Int	21-35-0	29-41-1
Total Offense Plays-Yards	65-397	70-503
Fumble Returns-Yards	0-0	0-0
Punt Returns-Yards	0-0	2-0
Kickoff Returns-Yards	4-57	5-105
Interception Returns-Yards	1-0	0-0
Punts (Number-Avg)	5-44.4	3-38.0
Fumbles-Lost	1-0	2-2
Sacks By (Number-Yards)	1-5	4-33
Penalties-Yards	5-45	4-50
Possession Time	28:58	29:51

The Buckeyes made plays when they had to, though. After the third turnover, a second fumbled snap between center Doug Datish and Smith, they forced a three-and-out.

Taking over on the Ohio State 17-yard line, Smith directed an 11-play, 83-yard drive that all but clinched it. The key moment came on third-and-15 from the Michigan 38, when Smith rolled right and threw incomplete but was hit helmet to helmet by linebacker Shawn Crable.

The personal foul penalty gave the Buckeyes a first down. Three plays later, Smith found Brian Robiskie from 13 yards to make it 42-31.

Michigan drove for a score and a two-point conversion with 2:16 remaining, but the ensuing onside kick landed in Ginn's arms to seal it.

Next up is the wait to see who OSU will face as it tries for its sixth national title. But that's then.

For now, the Buckeyes just wanted to bask in their victory in what was billed as the greatest game in the history of the teams' rivalry.

"All you do is throw your hands up and just say 'Thanks, God,' as you walk off the field," Ginn said. "I'm one of the luckiest, happiest men in the world."

Jay Richardson (99) sacks Michigan QB Chad Henne in the second half. Henne was sacked four times during the game.
Dispatch photo by Neal C. Lauron

SMITH'S TOUGHNESS PLAYS KEY ROLE, TRUMPS MICHIGAN

BY BOB HUNTER

The solution to the mystery of Ohio State's recent mastery of Michigan began with an incomplete pass in the fourth quarter.

On second-and-10 from the Michigan 33-yard line, Troy Smith got leveled from the blind side by a bullet train named LaMarr Woodley. Smith's pass to Ted Ginn Jr. fell incomplete, and in a 35-31 game, the crowd must have experienced a brief moment of panic.

Up popped Smith like a man made of indestructible elastic, and after a 5-yard penalty, the Ohio State quarterback rolled to his right on third-and-15. As he neared the sideline—wham!—a Smith-seeking missile name Shawn Crable rammed the fifth-year senior helmet to helmet, the kind of blow that should have left Smith thinking he was a riding on a fast merry-go-round.

Instead, he bounced up again as if he had merely tripped on that shaky sod, eager to see whether his pass had been completed—it wasn't—but happy to benefit from a 15-yard roughing-the-passer penalty.

By now, you probably know where this is going. No worse for wear, the indestructible one completed an 8-yard pass to Brian Robiskie on the next play, ran 2 yards for the first down on the next

Troy Smith and Ted Ginn Jr. celebrate Ginn's 39-yard touchdown reception in the second quarter against Michigan. *Dispatch photo by Mike Munden*

play and then hit Roblskie again for a 13-yard touchdown pass that proved to be the winner in a 42-39 Ohio State victory.

As a starting quarterback, Smith is 3-0 against Michigan. It is hardly a coincidence.

"For however many years we've been talking about Troy, his No. 1 quality is his toughness," Ohio State coach Jim Tressel said. "If you want to be a champion as quarterback, toughness is No. 1, and he is that."

Tressel is 5-1 against Michigan. That will lead to even more questions about what manner of genius this man brought to an Ohio State football program that couldn't have won this game under John Cooper for most of the '90s with the 1972 Miami Dolphins disguised as Buckeyes.

With all due respect to Tressel, who has obviously had a lot to do with this, three of his five wins have come with Smith at quarterback. Smith takes no credit for this, which is nice, but it is the kind of stuff that should frankly be left on the campaign trail.

He had a first half that would have defined some Ohio State quarterbacks' careers against Michigan—21 of 26 for 241 yards and three touchdowns—but the momentum turned in part because of his receivers' drops. He was sacked only once, but he was hit repeatedly by an aggressive Michigan defense an instant after he released the ball. He didn't wince once.

"I come back to the huddle and I stare at 10 guys in the huddle, eyes wide open, alert and ready to dominate the opposing team," Smith said. "I go to the sideline and there's 105-plus guys, eyes wide open and ready to do any and every thing they can in support of our team.

"So there's no way I can get to a situation where I feel as if my leg is hurt, my knee is hurt, my elbow is hurt and limp up or act like something's wrong with my body. Because I've been in situations where I see scout team players constantly beat their bodies up, play and play and play after play. So I never shortchange any of my teammates."

It is a strange choice of words—shortchange—from a man who in all probability is a lock to win the Heisman Trophy, because it seems almost certain that this 12-0 team wouldn't be heading the national championship game without him. He is the only quarterback in school history to have started and won three games against Michigan.

"I've said it time and time again," Smith said. "It's not me beating Michigan. It's the team that lined up and took the field every year that I got to start as quarterback that beat Michigan. They're also 3-0."

Well, maybe.

But think Cooper wouldn't like to have had a go against Michigan with Smith in his backfield?

> ## "FOR HOWEVER MANY YEARS WE'VE BEEN TALKING ABOUT TROY, HIS NO. 1 QUALITY IS HIS TOUGHNESS. IF YOU WANT TO BE A CHAMPION AS QUARTERBACK, TOUGHNESS IS NO. 1, AND HE IS THAT."
>
> BUCKEYES COACH JIM TRESSEL

Head coach Jim Tressel embraces quarterback Troy Smith as Ohio State's senior players were celebrated before their game with Michigan. *Dispatch photo by Jeff Hinckley*

Dispatch photo by Karl Kuntz

INDIVIDUAL STATS

SCORING	TD	FGs	(PATs) Kick	(PATs) Rush	(PATs) Rcv	(PATs) Pass	Points
Pittman, Antonio	13	0-0	0-0	0-0	0	0-0	78
Pettrey, Aaron	0	8-11	53-56	0-0	0	0-0	77
Ginn Jr., Ted	10	0-0	0-0	0-0	0	0-0	60
Gonzalez, Anthony	8	0-0	0-0	0-0	0	0-0	48
Wells, Chris	7	0-0	0-0	0-0	0	0-0	42
Robiskie, Brian	5	0-0	0-0	0-0	0	0-0	30
Nicol, Rory	3	0-0	0-0	0-0	0	0-0	18
Hall, Roy	2	0-0	0-0	0-0	0	0-0	12
Hartline, Brian	2	0-0	0-0	0-0	0	0-0	12
Smith, Antonio	1	0-0	0-0	0-0	0	0-0	6
Ballard, Jake	1	0-0	0-0	0-0	0	0-0	6
Wells, Maurice	1	0-0	0-0	0-0	0	0-0	6
Small, Ray	1	0-0	0-0	0-0	0	0-0	6
Mitchell, Brandon	1	0-0	0-0	0-0	0	0-0	6
Boeckman, Todd	1	0-0	0-0	0-0	0	0-0	6
Jenkins, Malcolm	1	0-0	0-0	0-0	0	0-0	6
Zwick, Justin	1	0-0	0-0	0-0	0	0-0	6
Smith, Troy	1	0-0	0-0	0-0	0	0-0	6
Pretorius, Ryan	0	1-2	2-2	0-0	0	0-0	5
Trapasso, A.J.	0	0-0	0-0	0-1	0	0-0	0
Total	59	9-13	55-58	0-1	0	0-0	436
Opponents	14	9-12	12-12	0-1	1	1-1	125

TOTAL OFFENSE	G	Plays	Rush	Pass	Total	Avg/G
Smith, Troy	12	359	233	2507	2740	228.3
Pittman, Antonio	12	232	1171	0	1171	97.6
Wells, Chris	12	102	567	0	567	47.2
Zwick, Justin	7	25	-1	187	186	26.6
Wells, Maurice	12	46	171	0	171	14.2
Ginn Jr., Ted	12	5	17	38	55	4.6
Boeckman, Todd	3	7	14	19	33	11.0
Gonzalez, Anthony	12	2	28	0	28	2.3
Schoenhoft, Rob	2	2	-19	5	-14	-7.0
TEAM	12	3	-20	0	-20	-1.7
Total	12	783	2161	2756	4917	409.8
Opponents	12	719	1122	2154	3276	273.0

RUSHING	GP	Att	Gain	Loss	Net	Avg	TD	Long	Avg/G
Pittman, Antonio	12	232	1209	38	1171	5.0	13	56	97.6
Wells, Chris	12	102	578	11	567	5.6	7	52	47.2
Smith, Troy	12	62	312	79	233	3.8	1	34	19.4
Wells, Maurice	12	46	176	5	171	3.7	1	32	14.2
Gonzalez, Anthony	12	2	29	1	28	14.0	0	29	2.3
Ginn Jr., Ted	12	3	23	6	17	5.7	0	16	1.4
Boeckman, Todd	3	4	14	0	14	3.5	1	5	4.7
Zwick, Justin	7	2	1	2	-1	-0.5	1	1	-0.1
Schoenhoft, Rob	2	1	0	19	-19	-19.0	0	0	-9.5
TEAM	12	3	0	20	-20	-6.7	0	0	-1.7
Total	12	457	2342	181	2161	4.7	24	56	180.1
Opponents	12	341	1487	365	1122	3.3	6	54	93.5

PASSING	GP	Effic	Cmp-Att-Int	Pct	Yds	TD	Long	Avg/G
Smith, Troy	12	167.87	199-297-5	67.0	2507	30	58	208.9
Zwick, Justin	7	129.17	14-23-0	60.9	187	0	36	26.7
Boeckman, Todd	3	119.87	2-3-0	66.7	19	0	12	6.3
Ginn Jr., Ted	12	374.60	1-2-0	50.0	38	1	38	3.2
Schoenhoft, Rob	2	142.00	1-1-0	100.0	5	0	5	2.5
Total	12	165.89	217-326-5	66.6	2756	31	58	229.7
Opponents	12	100.88	216-378-21	57.1	2154	8	65	179.5

RECEIVING	GP	No.	Yds	Avg	TD	Long	Avg/G
Ginn Jr., Ted	12	59	781	13.2	9	58	65.1
Gonzalez, Anthony	12	49	723	14.8	8	33	60.2
Robiskie, Brian	12	29	383	13.2	5	39	31.9
Hartline, Brian	12	16	243	15.2	2	32	20.2
Nicol, Rory	12	13	151	11.6	3	38	12.6
Hall, Roy	10	13	147	11.3	2	27	14.7
Pittman, Antonio	12	13	116	8.9	0	30	9.7
Small, Ray	10	8	68	8.5	1	36	6.8
White Jr., Stan	12	8	57	7.1	0	11	4.8
Wells, Maurice	12	3	55	18.3	0	30	4.6
Wells, Chris	12	2	16	8.0	0	10	1.3
Dukes, Albert	7	2	11	5.5	0	12	1.6
Ballard, Jake	9	2	5	2.5	1	4	0.6
Total	12	217	2756	12.7	31	58	229.7
Opponents	12	216	2154	10.0	8	65	179.5

PUNT RETURNS	No.	Yds	Avg	TD	Long
Ginn Jr., Ted	24	266	11.1	1	60
Jenkins, Malcolm	2	7	3.5	0	2
Grant, Larry	1	9	9.0	0	0
Gonzalez, Anthony	1	11	11.0	0	11
Robiskie, Brian	1	0	0.0	0	0
Total	29	293	10.1	1	60
Opponents	11	91	8.3	0	34

KICK RETURNS	No.	Yds	Avg	TD	Long
Ginn Jr., Ted	17	347	20.4	0	37
Gonzalez, Anthony	4	42	10.5	0	16
O'Neal, Jamario	2	48	24.0	0	31
Hall, Roy	1	21	21.0	0	21
Total	24	458	19.1	0	37
Opponents	41	741	18.1	0	53

FUMBLE RETURNS	No.	Yds	Avg	TD	Long
Washington, Donald	1	48	48.0	0	48
Total	1	48	48.0	0	48
Opponents	0	0	0.0	0	0

INTERCEPTIONS	No.	Yds	Avg	TD	Long
Laurinaitis, James	5	56	11.2	0	25
Jenkins, Malcolm	4	99	24.8	0	61
Freeman, Marcus	2	5	2.5	0	5
Mitchell, Brandon	2	59	29.5	1	46
Smith, Antonio	2	63	31.5	1	55
O'Neal, Jamario	1	0	0.0	0	0
Grant, Larry	1	49	49.0	0	49
Homan, Ross	1	5	5.0	0	5
Gholston, Vernon	1	8	8.0	0	8
Amos, Andre	1	-2	-2.0	0	0
Russell, Anderson	1	0	0.0	0	0
Total	21	342	16.3	3	61
Opponents	5	0	0.0	0	0

FIELD GOALS	FGM-FGA	Pct	01-19	20-29	30-39	40-49	50-99	Lg	Blk
Pretorius, Ryan	1-2	50.0	0-0	0-0	0-0	0-0	1-2	52	0
Pettrey, Aaron	8-11	72.7	0-0	0-1	3-3	3-4	2-3	51	0

PUNTING	No.	Yds	Avg	Long	TB	FC	I20	Blkd
Trapasso, A.J.	43	1763	41.0	60	4	8	15	0
Total	43	1763	41.0	60	4	8	15	0
Opponents	73	2804	38.4	68	6	9	22	1

KICKOFFS	No.	Yds	Avg	TB	OB	Retn	Net	YdLn
Pettrey, Aaron	61	3826	62.7	35	0			
Pretorius, Ryan	19	1153	60.7	3	0			
Total	80	4979	62.2	38	0	741	43.5	21
Opponents	32	1821	56.9	7	0	458	38.2	26

OVERALL DEFENSIVE STATISTICS

	GP	(Tackles) Solo	(Tackles) Ast	Total	TFL/Yds	(Sacks) No-Yds	Int-Yds	(Pass) BrUp	QBH	(Fumbles) Rcv-Yds	(Fumbles) FF	Blocked Kicks
Laurinaitis, James	12	43	57	100	8.5-44	4.0-40	5-56	1	-	-	3	-
Smith, Antonio	12	38	28	66	10.0-51	2.0-28	2-63	1	1	1-0	1	-
Freeman, Marcus	12	25	31	56	2.5-8	1.0-6	2-5	6	-	-	-	-
Jenkins, Malcolm	12	37	14	51	2.5-8	-	4-99	3	1	-	1	-
Mitchell, Brandon	12	28	23	51	3.0-8	-	2-59	4	-	2-0	-	-
Gholston, Vernon	12	19	25	44	14.0-79	7.5-66	1-8	1	1	-	-	-
Pitcock, Quinn	11	19	17	36	11.0-47	8.0-42	-	-	1	-	-	-
Washington, Donald	12	22	12	34	1.0-3	-	-	1	1	1-48	2	-
Homan, Ross	12	15	13	28	2.0-15	1.0-13	1-5	-	-	-	-	-
Kerr, John	12	7	19	26	1.5-1	-	-	1	-	-	-	-
O'Neal, Jamario	12	11	13	24	0.5-4	0.5-4	1-0	1	-	-	-	-
Richardson, Jay	12	15	9	24	8.5-26	4.0-17	-	7	2	1-0	-	-
Patterson, David	11	6	12	18	3.0-5	-	-	1	1	-	-	-
Grant, Larry	11	8	10	18	0.5-3	0.5-3	1-49	2	-	-	1	1
Terry, Curtis	12	8	9	17	3.5-7	-	-	2	1	1-0	1	-
Penton, Joel	12	5	12	17	3.0-20	2.0-14	-	-	-	-	-	-
Russell, Anderson	5	8	8	16	1.0-1	-	1-0	-	-	-	-	-
Wilson, Lawrence	10	6	8	14	5.0-17	3.0-15	-	1	1	-	2	-
Gant, Aaron	7	7	3	10	-	-	-	-	-	-	1	-
Hartline, Brian	12	7	2	9	-	-	-	-	-	-	-	-
Coleman, Kurt	11	5	4	9	0.5-1	-	-	-	-	-	-	1
Amos, Andre	10	4	5	9	-	-	1-2	1	-	-	-	-
Spitler, Austin	12	3	4	7	-	-	-	-	-	-	-	-
Barrow, Alex	11	4	3	7	1.0-2	-	-	-	-	-	-	-
Rose, Robert	8	5	2	7	3.5-23	3.5-23	-	-	-	-	-	-
TEAM	12	3	3	6	-	-	-	-	-	-	-	-
Lane, Shaun	12	5	1	6	-	-	-	-	-	-	-	-
Patterson, Nick	12	2	3	5	-	-	-	-	-	-	-	-
Denlinger, Todd	10	2	2	4	2.0-4	-	-	-	-	-	-	-
Smith, Brandon	8	1	2	3	-	-	-	-	-	-	-	-
Worthington, Doug	7	2	1	3	-	-	-	-	-	-	-	-
Pettrey, Aaron	12	2	1	3	-	-	-	-	-	-	-	-
Harden, Derek	8	2	1	3	-	-	-	-	-	-	-	-
Norman, Drew	12	-	1	1	-	-	-	-	-	-	-	-
Rehring, Steve	12	1	-	1	-	-	-	-	-	-	-	-
Larson, J.D.	3	1	-	1	-	-	-	-	-	-	-	-
Potokar, Dan	3	-	1	1	-	-	-	-	-	-	-	-
Robinson, Trevor	12	-	1	1	-	-	-	-	-	-	-	-
Datish, Doug	12	1	-	1	-	-	-	-	-	-	-	-
White Jr., Stan	12	-	1	1	-	-	-	-	-	-	-	-
Small, Ray	10	-	1	1	-	-	-	-	-	-	-	-
Hall, Roy	10	1	-	1	-	-	-	-	-	-	-	-
Ginn Jr., Ted	12	1	-	1	-	-	-	-	-	-	-	-
Total	12	379	362	741	88-377	37-271	21-342	33	10	6-48	12	2
Opponents	12	433	444	877	49-176	14-95	5-0	24	15	11-0	9	2

TEAM STATS

	OSU	OPP
SCORING	436	125
Points Per Game	36.3	10.4
FIRST DOWNS	253	181
Rushing	112	63
Passing	134	104
Penalty	7	14
RUSHING YARDAGE	2161	1122
Yards Gained Rushing	2342	1487
Yards Lost Rushing	181	365
Rushing Attempts	457	341
Average Per Rush	4.7	3.3
Average Per Game	180.1	93.5
TDs Rushing	24	6
PASSING YARDAGE	2756	2154
Att-Comp-Int	326-217-5	378-216-21
Average Per Pass	8.5	5.7
Average Per Catch	12.7	10.0
Average Per Game	229.7	179.5
TDs Passing	31	8
TOTAL OFFENSE	4917	3276
Total Plays	783	719
Average Per Play	6.3	4.6
Average Per Game	409.8	273.0
KICK RETURNS: #-YARDS	24-458	41-741
PUNT RETURNS: #-YARDS	29-293	11-91
INT RETURNS: #-YARDS	21-342	5-0
KICK RETURN AVERAGE	19.1	18.1
PUNT RETURN AVERAGE	10.1	8.3
INT RETURN AVERAGE	16.3	0.0
FUMBLES–LOST	17-11	19-6

	OSU	OPP
PENALTIES–YARDS	57-514	43-337
Average Per Game	42.8	28.1
PUNTS–YARDS	43-1763	73-2804
Average Per Punt	41.0	38.4
Net Punt Average	37.0	32.8
TIME OF POSSESSION/GAME	31:46	28:00
3rd-DOWN CONVERSIONS	77/150	48/157
3rd-Down Pct	51%	31%
4th-DOWN CONVERSIONS	7/10	8/14
4th-Down Pct	70%	57%
SACKS BY–YARDS	37-271	14-95
MISC YARDS	14	0
TOUCHDOWNS SCORED	59	14
FIELD GOALS–ATTEMPTS	9-13	9-12
ON-SIDE KICKS	0-0	0-2
RED-ZONE SCORES	44-52 85%	21-25 84%
RED-ZONE TOUCHDOWNS	40-52 77%	12-25 48%
PAT-ATTEMPTS	55-58 95%	12-12 100%
ATTENDANCE	735674	333986
Games/Avg Per Game	7/105096	5/66797

SCORE BY QUARTERS	1st	2nd	3rd	4th	TOTAL
Ohio State	111	133	75	117	436
Opponents	20	37	20	48	125

Dispatch photo by Craig Holman

Celebrate Ohio sports in these other great books from Sports Publishing!

Game of My Life: Ohio State
ISBN: 1582618216
Price: $24.95
Author: Steve Greenberg and Laura Lanese

Learn about the greatest game in the lives of several former Ohio State football players. Players include: Ken Kuhn, Archie Griffin, Jack Tatum, Jim Lachey.

Tales from the Cleveland Cavaliers
ISBN: 1582618399
Price: $19.95
Author: Roger Gordon, Foreword by Austin Carr

Enjoy the anecdotes about this special rookie and rare commodity-plus therest of the Cavaliers, from celebrations on the day of the lottery to LeBron's debut.

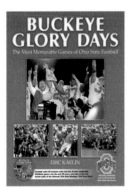

Buckeye Glory Days
ISBN: 1582616817
Price: $29.95
Author: Eric Kaelin

The author of this book captures the great moments in Ohio State football history with the radio calls from the games on a 75 minute compact disc/book combination.

Uncaged
ISBN: 1596700424
Price: $24.95
Author: David Krider and J.R. Shelt

The never-before-told story of some of the top high school basketball players in the nation. Greg Oden and Mike Conley take the basketball program by storm and were both recruited by Ohio State in 2006.

Ohio State's Unforgetables
ISBN: 1582612439
Price: $29.95
Author: Bruca Hooley

This is the story of the Ohio State's undefeated run to the 1968 national championship. For the Ohio State loyalists, there hasn't been a time like the 10-0-0 sweep in '68.

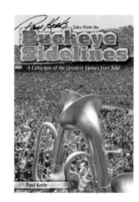

Paul Keels' Tales from the Buckeye's Championship Season
ISBN: 158261539X
Price: $19.95
Author: Paul Keels

The 2002 team was picked by many to place third at best in the Big Ten. But behind a rock-solid defense, outstanding special teams and other great players, Ohio State grabbed college football's top prize. Read the stories that made it all happen.

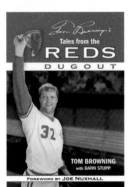

Tom Browning's Tales from the Reds
ISBN: 1596700467
Price: $19.95
Author: Tom Browning with Dann Stupp

Fans can join Cincinnati Reds Hall of Fame pitcher Tom Browning for legendary tales of festivity, a perfect game, and life with Marge Schott.

To place an order 24-hours-a-day, please call toll-free **1-877-424-BOOK (2665)**.
You can also order online by visiting us at *www.SportsPublishingLLC.com*.